A HOME FOR ALL SEASONS

A HOME FOR ALL SEASONS

GRACIOUS LIVING & STYLISH ENTERTAINING

DANIELLE ROLLINS

WRITTEN WITH MARIO LÓPEZ-CORDERO
FOREWORD BY MILES REDD
PRINCIPAL PHOTOGRAPHY BY LESLEY UNRUH
ADDITIONAL PHOTOGRAPHY BY SARAH DORIO AND MATTHEW MEAD

To my mother, Jan Deaton,
with love

Contents

Foreword

I met Danielle Rollins what seems a lifetime ago. I got a call out of the blue, and this charming voice told me the story of a house she loved in Atlanta. She would take walks in the afternoon, gazing at its majestic facade, and dream and dream and dream. One day, she put a note in the mailbox of its then-owner, on what I am sure was beautifully monogrammed stationery, asking if they would ever sell. As destiny would have it, the house soon became hers. This little tale gives you, dear reader, insight into the nature of Madame Rollins: she pursues the things she loves, and with determined patience she usually gets them.

Turns out, the manor in question was the extraordinary Boxwood House, a Georgian-Regency fantasy of the brilliant architect Philip Trammell Shutze and, as fate would have it, one of my favorite houses from childhood. Growing up in Atlanta, I was not averse to driving by the house with binoculars. I do believe that people get the houses that are meant for them, and Danielle was certainly meant to be the lady to breathe new life into this sleeping beauty, with me as her trusty decorator and general counsel.

Fast-forward many years that brought a new start, a new house, a new dog, and definitely a new lease on life, and Danielle has emerged as a modern-day renaissance woman: decorator, fashion designer, and entertaining guru. Though the truth is that she has always been those things. I think she just needed a gentle nudge, which she graciously gives me credit for encouraging. There is very little she cannot do, which is obvious from these beautiful pages. Her creativity and energy are astounding. She takes pleasure in life and masters everything with maddening swiftness, including haute French cuisine. She could practically give a master class in lampshades. In her deft hands, a Sheetrock-covered windowless basement transforms into a tented Hudson's Bay blanket fantasy. She mixes high and low, rough and refined, rigid and organic—sometimes, it seems, with a flute of pink champagne in hand. Danielle loves atmosphere and creates it wherever she goes, and atmosphere transcends decorating. It is a roaring fire of woodsy-smelling birch logs and a crisp white cloth on a candlelit table. It is the tactile and the ephemeral; I have even known her to whip up a cheese soufflé at midnight in a ball gown. In other words, the Auntie Mame gene runs very deep.

The new house, and the wonderful life Danielle has nurtured in it, is the focus of this book, and *oh* the inspiration it gives. You may just find yourself planning a boxwood parterre, having an alfresco dinner for twenty, or maybe, just maybe, whipping up that midnight soufflé. Alas, we can't all be Danielle, but these pages will certainly inspire you to live with greater zest and exuberance, and if that is not good enough reason to read a book, well, I can't think of a better one.

—Miles Redd

PLEASE JOIN

Daniella

FOR

a Garden dinner

ON

September 14, 2010

AT

Home
7pm

Introduction

Houses are so much more than the cement, brick, and wood they're made of. We invest them with so much meaning. They're status symbols, sanctuaries, showpieces. Stage sets for the drama plays of our lives. Ports in storms, party centrals, cloisters. They're full of life one day and empty nests the next. They'll stop your heart, break your heart, and stitch it back together. Sometimes you want to build them up. Sometimes you want to tear them down.

The houses in my life have been the cause of all of the above at some point or another, and the house in these pages came at an important turning point in my life. My marriage had ended, and this house was what happened in the aftermath. Rebuilding it helped me to rebuild my life. And not only because it gave me something to do, though there is great wisdom in the idea that if you want to get over something painful, one of the best methods for doing so is rolling up your shirtsleeves and getting to work. It cured me because it was a powerful reminder that the whole point of life is to share it with the people you love. I put so much work and effort into this project, and the moments when I enjoy it the most are when I'm sharing it. With my kids and parents, of course, but also with a great parade of loved ones and friends.

That, right there is the bright, warm truth at the center of the concept of entertaining. It's not some fluffy exercise you do to show off or save face or schmooze strangers (well, it *can* be—anyone can hire a caterer and throw a party—but people who do it like that are missing the boat and probably not having very much fun). What it is in a nutshell, is a way of living your life and a vehicle for sharing that life with gratitude and generosity.

And I'm here to tell you the secret to it all. It's really not that complicated. If a house is just a backdrop for breaking bread and clinking glasses and fireside heart-to-hearts—among a million other come-on-in scenarios—then there are ways of designing and running it that will make welcoming people in feel joyful and relatively stress-free. I got to start from scratch with this house, so I very deliberately crafted a home base conducive to that kind of life. I thought about architecture that could bend easily both to crowds at a big party and to intimate gatherings of family or friends, that would allow for the free flow of traffic in either situation, and that would eliminate the kind of dead-zone rooms that sap the soul right out of a house. I imagined purpose-driven spaces—the pool cabana, the sunroom—that could also accommodate imaginative out-of-the-box entertaining. I created self-contained rooms for my kids that could also function as guest suites when they eventually fly the coop.

Then I went a step further, because all that planning would be for naught if I couldn't actually *run* the house and fulfill my life-is-a-moveable-feast ambitions efficiently and effectively. These days, service areas like mud halls and butler's pantries tend to get short shrift because they feel like remnants of the past; yet modern interpretations of those very spaces are the backbone of my house because they make all the legwork you have to do to throw a party, cook dinner for friends, or host overnight guests feel seamless. *True* luxury is a laundry room that can handle an army! Building an infrastructure for storage and organization—open shelving for china and accessories, cabinets and drawers in which you don't have to root endlessly for a sheet pan or saucepan, linen closets designed to service specific rooms—won't just make your day-to-day life a hell of a lot easier, it will make you the kind of hostess that can turn out a sense of occasion at the drop of a hat.

Honestly, happy entertaining is also a habit, like making the bed. Have candles stocked, music at the ready, and cocktail napkins starched—I like to do it while I watch TV! If you keep your house relatively pulled together as a matter of course, then someone stopping by for an impromptu drink or dinner doesn't seem like such a big deal because you don't feel as if you have to put on a show every time a visitor walks through the front door.

And do you know how nice it is to offer family or friends a guest room instead of recommending a good hotel? (Or how nice it is to stay in a house where someone understands and recognizes the difference?) I keep entire shelves of closets devoted just to fresh-wrapped soaps in colors that coordinate to towels in a particular room. I have robes, charging cords, notepads with cups of pens, extra tissues, magazines and books, bottles of water, and cookies. And no, you don't have to get that obsessive about it, but you do see my point, don't you?

In the following pages, I'll take you on a room-by-room tour of the haven I created, starting with the driveway and ending in the backyard. Along the way, I'll share all the architecture, design, decorating, and entertaining tips that make running the kind of home people love to hang out in feel like second nature. I won't pretend it's snap-your-fingers easy, but it's not rocket science, either.

One more caveat before we get started. Here's what houses and entertaining should never be: perfect. If the last few years have taught me one thing, it's that life isn't perfect. And seriously, I can't imagine anything more boring. If you're looking for perfect here, close this book, put it back on the table or shelf where you found it, and walk away. We can part as friends, and I promise I won't hold it against you, if you don't hold it against me. But if you're looking instead for a primer on how to run your home and share it with the people you love in a meaningful, stylish way, imperfections be damned, then grab yourself a cup of coffee—or better yet, make a cockatil or pour a glass of wine—and get comfy. I promise we're going to have a good time.

First Impressions

If you could only have seen what my forlorn future dream house looked like from the street when I first laid eyes on it. *Wild* doesn't quite cover it. A once-manicured front yard had gone positively feral, a tangle of ivy, kudzu, and honeysuckle-covered scrub trees, it had grown so thick that the house itself was barely visible. The only driveway, which ran down the side of the house, looked like something out of Washington Irving: an eerie green tunnel overhung with shrubs, vines, and branches. It was a setting for a Gothic novel, not a refuge on one of the best streets in one of the most desirable neighborhoods in Atlanta.

But something in all that untamed neglect spoke to me. It was as if the house couldn't—*wouldn't*—be contained. I was starting a new chapter in my life, and I felt like I was meeting a kindred spirit, an overlooked diamond in the rough in which no one else but me could envision potential. In my mind's eye, I cleared away the overgrowth to reveal a Georgian facade—not the greatest architectural iteration of the style ever produced, but elegant nevertheless. The house was a Cinderella story waiting to be told, and I knew I was the right person to turn the fairy tale into real life—and maybe repair myself in the process.

I imagined a new driveway, aligned with the house's center axis and better in tune with its architecture, because the key to making almost anything pleasing to the eye is symmetry. I plotted out a motor court, sheltered by hedges and a low wall in the spirit of a cloister, large enough to function both for my family and for the guests I wanted to breeze through the new front door. (Parking is a perennial logistical problem when you're hosting in a car town.) One by one, the visions came: A carriage house–style garage addition that could double as a

OPPOSITE: I couldn't resist a portrait with my all-time dream car, a pristine restored navy blue Ferrari Dino that a friend loaned to me; I had so many well-thought-out excuses to convince him I should keep it, from the fact that navy blue is one of my favorite colors to how well the shade would have meshed with the driveway!
ABOVE: Vintage wrought-iron garden furniture was powder-coated in a deep navy shade to match shutters painted in Benjamin Moore's Polo Blue. That kind of cohesion is a great way to make a facade and entryway look shipshape and polished.

service wing for back-of-house tasks (and that would connect to the kitchen so unloading groceries wasn't so much of a chore). A fresh coat of white paint on the facade. Working shutters in a crisp shade of navy blue. An allée of crape myrtle leading to a front gate and a small parterre garden that would be a graceful backdrop to parties I could have in what was essentially the driveway. Crape myrtle is considered a down-market plant in the South and people might balk at the idea of hosting a party in my driveway, but telling me that something is "not done" is a surefire way to get me to figure out how to do it.

Making the fantasy a reality took some ingenuity. To clear the overgrowth, I found a farmer in northern Georgia who trucked in a herd of twenty goats (my new neighbors wanted to kill me, but it worked like a charm). In order for the motor court to work, we had to haul in literally tons of dirt and build a retaining wall. My friend, and architect Bill Ingram, conceived a showstopping garage with room for a guest suite above and a central tower designed to look like a dovecote, complete with a stepped brick pattern. I obsessed over a front gate with a windmill chinoiserie Chippendale pattern and went back and forth with the ironworker to get it right. I used spray paint and tape to mark out the boxwood garden for the landscapers, and it was a great way to get a feel for the actual dimensions of the finished product. We raised the front entry to give it more of a sense of occasion and replaced the front door with a center-knob version, then lacquered it a deep teal blue. Larger traditional sash windows (complete with weighted pulleys) on the first and second floors gave the house even more symmetry and flooded the interiors with extra light. Cedar shingles on the roof completed a miraculous face-lift.

The experience of a house really starts at the curb. As they say, you never get a second chance to make a first impression. Today, when you pull off the street and crunch into the driveway, you're really walking into the first room of my house. The crape myrtles are like a hallway with wallpaper that changes with the seasons—all blooms and greens in spring and summer, statuesque and sculptural in the winter (with gorgeously colored pale wood that shows up on the bare trunks once the bark has shed). The gate swings wide, you pull into the sheltered motor court, and you're already a million miles away from the busy thoroughfare. The cheery front door beckons you inside. The effect, I'm thrilled to report, is now way more Jane Austen than Washington Irving.

ABOVE AND PREVIOUS PAGES: The house's original red brick was whitewashed in Benjamin Moore's Cloud White mixed with sand, an old painter's trick for adding texture and an instant aged look.
OPPOSITE: The garage was modeled after a carriage house with a dovecote-esque central bay, complete with a stepped brick pattern.

PREVIOUS PAGES: Painting your front door a bright, happy color is the decorating equivalent of shouting "Hello!" RIGHT: The service wing, which includes a mud hall and has direct access to the garden, connects the garage to the kitchen so I don't have to trek through the house to unload groceries. I mapped out a plan for the boxwood pattern garden using spray paint directly on the soil to preview and tweak the design to perfection.

(*Stylish Entertaining*)
A TOAST TO THE HOUSE

You've heard of birthday celebrations for people and pets, but singing "Happy Birthday" to a house? Well, why not? It was two years to the day that I'd herded in those goats to clear out the overgrown landscape, and when I realized that, I knew I wanted to commemorate it. The house—and I—had come such a long way. Sometimes you need a minute to take stock and be grateful for how far you've come. I'll make almost any excuse to throw a party, but gratitude is one of life's best reasons to do *anything*.

The motor court was an unexpected venue, but I'm a sucker for hosting gatherings in surprising places. It gives you a fresh perspective, allowing you to appreciate an environment from a new angle, and shakes up the expected formula of sitting around a table in a dining room. From a spot in front of the parterre garden, we could admire the house itself and revel in what was going to be a spectacular sunset—a substitute for the standard chandelier and candles that can't be beat.

It came together very last minute, with four close friends who were easy to corral on short notice (my favorite kind of gathering). I keep several Coleman folding camping tables around precisely because they're so easy to move and you can use multiples in a variety of configurations—a long table, a big square, a bar. Throw a tablecloth over them, and they look like a million bucks. I pulled a couple up to a wrought-iron bench that sits in the driveway and gathered outdoor chairs from elsewhere in the garden.

The tablecloth was a gift from a thoughtful friend who'd had it made from a vintage Liberty of London print fabric I used in my first fashion collection. It set the blue-and-white color scheme, which I followed up with Mottahedeh plates—first firings of their iconic Tobacco Leaf pattern, which I bought in bulk at a sample sale. (The patterns were deemed too flawed for subsequent colors, but they have an abstract beauty that I love.) An ikat-patterned telephone table from the family room matched the palette, so I brought it outside to use as a serving board. If you limit yourself to only outdoor pieces outside, you are missing out, because indoor furnishings in the open air bring a sense of occasion to anything they touch, including takeout chicken salad and a bakery-bought coconut cake, which I served with champagne to pair with my sparkling mood.

With the right props—layered tablecloths, porcelain place settings, hurricane lanterns, flatware, and flowers—you can throw a party anywhere, even in your front driveway. It's not accidental that the blue-and-white color combination mirrors the hues of the facade.

Making an Entrance

or entry halls, I have a somewhat contradictory design philosophy. When a guest first walks through your front door, they *should* get a certain kind of thrill. But I am not a big fan of the take-no-prisoners, shout-it-from-the-rooftops statement space, because they're just not human enough. Interiors like that are trying so hard to impress you that they just end up feeling cold. My previous house was so formal and grand that I was only ever comfortable surrounded by forty people at a party. Whenever it was just little ol' me waltzing in, it felt as if I were being swallowed whole. To me, front halls are transition points: they should gently herald the rooms to which they lead, but also feel warm and restful. You're in and out of the space every day—it needs to be welcoming. If an entry hall were a person, it'd be stylish and well dressed, sure, but it would also reach out and give you a big hug. My litmus test here, and throughout the house, really, was that if a design choice makes me feel like I have to wear shoes in the space, then we're not doing it. Is there anything better than approachable chic?

In my case, I applied a best-of-both-worlds strategy and started with the architecture. For drama, I created a classic enfilade running from the entryway to the back of the house by retrofitting an existing series of small spaces—some separated by doors—and topping it all off with a sunroom. Enfilades date from the palatial architecture of the Baroque period, in which a succession of rooms leads from one to another in a single sight line, implying luxury and grandeur along the way. I removed all the doors so that when you first walk into the house, your eye is instantly drawn through the parade of spaces to the sunroom and into the back garden beyond the windows. Drama factor, check.

OPPOSITE: As an axis point that connects the family room to the living room, the entry space bridges those rooms through color, playing up tones from marine blue to watery aqua shades that are present in both. ABOVE: A porcelain parrot roosts on an antique bracket in the sunroom, picking up the theme in the adjoining passageway, where the bird-themed wallpaper makes a major design statement.

A front hall needs to set the tone for the entire house, but it shouldn't take itself too seriously. Warm and welcoming is the order of the day.

But since the scale of the individual spaces in the enfilade were of a piece with one another and the rest of the house—meaning they were intimate and not too lofty—they didn't knock you over the head trying to impress you. Welcoming factor, check.

I kept the cased openings in between because I wanted to softly delineate the spaces according to function—without those openings, it would have looked like one long bowling alley. The first space is a classic foyer with direct access into the living and dining rooms to the left and right, respectively. Stylistically, I kept it quiet, so it doesn't compete with those other interiors—two of the biggest showstoppers in the house—and furnished it with a coral tole lantern, chinoiserie brackets holding Chinese porcelain jars, vintage bird prints framed with French mats, and velvet-covered X-base stools, great for slipping on or off shoes or stashing a handbag while you come in or go out.

The second space is actually a staircase landing serving the childrens' and guest rooms upstairs. It is a hub and needed to be equipped for function, so there's a Georgian console topped with silver trays and boxes to hold mail and keys, wallets, and phone chargers; a neoclassical mirror for last-minute checkups before heading out the door; and a dog bed for any one of the many in the menagerie. To differentiate it from the other spaces I wanted to cover the landing area with wallpaper, but a pattern would have been impossible because the staircase gave the ceiling way too many elevation changes. Instead, I layered the walls in a grasscloth and framed the edges and borders with Prussian-blue grosgrain ribbon applied with brass nailhead tacks. The effect is almost like moldings and highlights the wonky architecture in an appealing way. Sometimes the best solution to a design conundrum is just embracing it.

ABOVE AND OPPOSITE: A classic enfilade is the architectural backbone of the entry hall. Come in the front door and the view spills all the way to the back garden. Perpendicular axes also run through it, with sight lines that range from the living room to the dining room on one side and from the library to the kitchen on the other. See how tones and shades pop through and reappear in each respective space?

I subjected every space in the house to my barefoot test—if I didn't feel like I could waltz in wearing nothing on my feet then it was definitely a no go.

The next space, like the foyer, bridges the living and family rooms and is a pretty major thoroughfare in terms of the life of the house. At this point, you're within the inner sanctum, and unlike the foyer, I wanted this hallway to stand on its own. I think of it as my display window, like it's a shop on Main Street. A skirted library table holds court in its center and functions as a platform for a rotating selection of coffee-table books and seasonal displays of greenery and flowers—a potted topiary in the fall, poinsettias at Christmas, branches and blooms from the garden in spring and summer. Skirting the table also gives me another way of changing the vibe because I can switch out the skirt, just like I do with tablecloths in the dining room, to instantly modify the look. The main visual cue, however, is a whimsical wallpaper I just love. It echoes the framed bird prints in the foyer with a vibrant trompe l'oeil pattern of birds in frames, which connects the spaces in a tongue-in-cheek way.

The enfilade is capped by the sunroom, my Elsie de Wolfe moment and a destination in its own right. I wanted it to feel like the pool cabana or the garden. Cue the lattice! I took a page from de Wolfe's book and lined the ivory-painted room in wooden trellis I bought at Home Depot and had painted Prussian blue. It was *so* inexpensive and brings up a good point: not everything you decorate with has to be precious. If it were really pristine, like hand-forged iron trellis imported from France, it would have made the space too stuffy. As it is, it relaxes the mood. Throw in some overscale wicker armchairs, blue-and-white Chinese garden stools, and ficus trees in pots, and it's a divine place to unwind, especially in the winter. The room also accommodates a sixty-inch round table, so you better believe I'll set up a table in here if I'm only having a few people over for lunch or supper.

ABOVE: The central bay is a stair landing with access to bedrooms upstairs. Architectural renderings hung along the staircase feel like windows; grosgrain ribbon pinned with brass tacks acts as a molding. OPPOSITE: A Georgian console and mirror anchor a landing spot for keys. My cheat for lampshades is to buy off the rack and embellish with fringe, trim, or pompoms. No one can ever tell the difference.

Adding onto the back of the house gave me room for a sunroom that I wanted to feel like a formal cabana and a destination. It looks fancy, but the materials it's crafted from are decidedly not. I bought Home Depot lattice and plotted out panels and borders, then had it all lacquered and installed over the white walls.

THE COLOR BOUNCE

I call it the color bounce and it's one of my favorite games to play, whether I happen to be working on a design project or not. The object is to find a way to thread color and pattern through an entire house in a seamless way.

Here's the secret: as vivid as my house is, all its vibrancy really comes from twelve basic colors. It's just their tonality that changes, and those tonalities work with one another as long as you're mindful of their undertones: red and coral and orange all make a nice mix because they share the same base and have the same heat; ditto that for cool colors such as turquoise and Prussian blue. At the start of every project, I always ask a client to give me his or her twelve favorite colors, and these become the springboard for everything I do.

I know it might seem like a lot, but don't sweat mixing twelve colors together, even if they feel as far apart from one another as eggplant and spinach green—those two shades happen to look fabulous together in my dining room. Don't believe me? Look around the room you're currently sitting in. I guarantee you'll see more than twelve colors in that space alone. Narrowing down your shades to twelve actually gives you a very workable number. Secondly, as counterintuitive as it sounds, the more you add to the mix, the more forgiving the scheme becomes. Everything will go together more easily. A two-color room is not only harder to pull off, it also comes off as "decorated," not a look I think anyone should strive for. If you want an interior that feels personal, organic, and acquired over time, then the more the merrier.

Next comes the bouncing. What you want to do to make a palette cohesive across an entire house is to give the individual shades perches throughout the residence, "bouncing" them across paint, wallpaper, fabrics, artwork, tassels, brackets, porcelain—basically anything—in room after room.

In my case, the journey starts at the front door with its shiny Prussian-blue lacquer, a deep marine shade that is not too green and has just enough black in it to keep it from feeling too sweet—I love it so much that it's become my signature. So that hue goes from the front door onto baseboards in the foyer, hops onto one of the tones in a small-scale wallpaper on the ceiling, leaps to grosgrain-ribbon trim in the stair landing, takes a detour on the ikat-stripe fabric on the walls in the living room, reappears in bird-print wallpaper and baseboards in the part of the hall I think of as my "display window," is splashed all over the latticework and furnishings in the sunroom, and then basically marches all over the rest of the house in some form or another. As long as you're tempering the volume—a lot here and a little there, a little here and a lot there—it'll be subtle enough to work, pinkie-promise.

The secret to decorating in a way that feels organic, evolved, and personal is to choose a family of twelve basic colors and then stick to them, varying gradations and tones as you go and weaving in plenty of patterns.

A CHRISTMAS THAT'S NOT CLICHÉ

Traditionalists will blanch when I say this, but when I pull out all the stops for Christmas, I try to avoid the expected green-and-red scheme. I also don't own special Christmas china or only use napkins with embroidered holly sprigs or glasses etched with snowflakes, either. I just don't think you have to go there in your own home. My approach is simply to take the colors and tones already in the room and and mix in seasonal florals and greenery to make it all work out.

The inspiration for a Christmas lunch I hosted for a small group of friends in the sunroom was a tablecloth with a big swirling paisley pattern that's chockablock with blues, corals, beiges, rusts, periwinkles, and, yes, a bit of red and green—pulling in shades from the living room on one side and the family room on the other. Since it *is* Christmas, the table deserved a sense of occasion: vermeil-handled flatware, vibrant salad and dinner plates atop a charger, and statuesque crystal stemware. Napkins with a coral ikat pattern and paisley-patterned votive holders deepened the exotic theme.

Even though I'm not a fan of red and green, I'm certainly no Scrooge. Christmas is one of my favorite times of year. I always use plenty of what I adore about the season: the branches, berries, and blooms we've all come to expect at the holidays. My main ingredients were pine and magnolia branches, ilex berries, decorative cabbages, and amaryllis and red roses. I made two arrangements in wicker baskets that I posted on pedestals behind either side of the table, framing a signature wreath of branches and pine I designed for a company called Weston Farms (they sell it as "Danielle's Lark"). For the centerpiece I went all out, filling a big silver punch bowl with all of the above so it overflowed in a grand gesture. Wrapped and beribboned presents for my guests doubled as place cards, and I crowned each place setting with a little nutcracker ornament. Humbug who?

OPPOSITE AND FOLLOWING PAGES: The sunroom is the perfect bright, warm spot for a Christmas lunch. I blended traditional holiday materials like pine boughs and cones, magnolia leaves, amaryllis, and decorative cabbages, along with unexpected patterns like paisleys and ikats.

Room for Living

I like to think of my living room as Grand Central Station, South, give or take a few cushy perches. It's the center of my house, a key entry and exit point right off the foyer through which pretty much everyone has to pass at some point during the day, which is exactly how I planned it. There's nothing worse than a dead-zone room that no one ever steps a foot into except for parties or special events.

When it comes to living rooms, the best way to combat that is to make it a nexus point in the house's larger floor plan and then furnish it for maximum comfort and style to seduce people into lingering, lounging, reading, gossiping, napping, playing cards, doing a puzzle, watching the fire, having a drink, or putting their feet up—i.e., *living*. In my case, the living room is the first spot a guest entering the house is likely to snuggle into, since it's close to the front door and there are so many cozy landing pads that it practically demands you sit a spell. For my family, it's a major thoroughfare with access to the library; bar; master suite; dining, family room; sunroom; and the garden. As a mom, it means I can park myself in front of the fire in an armchair and I'm pretty much guaranteed to see one of my kids on his or her way in or out of the house. Inveigling them into a tête-à-tête, even if only for a minute or two, is never a hard sell. For me, using design to facilitate these kinds of interactions is the whole point—otherwise you're just set dressing.

Of course, all of the abovementioned qualities mean the living room doubles as an incredible setting for parties because the furniture plan is optimized for an efficient flow of traffic and there are plenty of inviting nooks and crannies for guests to mingle in. In fact, when I was plotting out the room, I wanted it to feel as cosseting for one person as

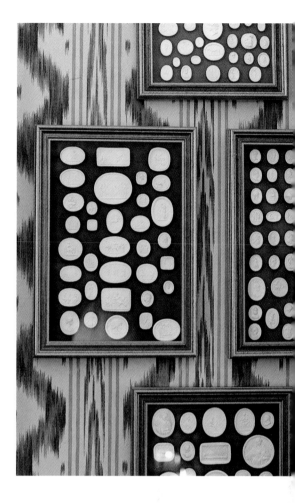

OPPOSITE AND FOLLOWING PAGES: The color scheme of the living room—and you might say the entire house—was inspired by the lush blues, greens, ochers, rusts, and terra-cottas in the gargantuan antique Oushak rug that's one of my most prized possessions. ABOVE: Treating objects as art and hanging them on the walls, like this collection of framed antique intaglios or porcelain elsewhere, gives a room incredible dimension and mementos with meaning pride of place.

The living room has multiple
entry points and only one jib door
that leads to the bar. I never put
doors in a room unless they're
totally necessary. You have to
focus on how they fall, and they
screw up the furniture plan.
They're like people who need to
talk when everyone else was fine
with the quiet. FOLLOWING PAGES:
The more you add to a room, the
more everything hangs together,
especially if you capitalize on
common themes like a chinoiserie mirror and secretary, a Louis
XV chest and armchair, and
fabrics in corresponding shades.
Just save room for the personal
and kooky, like pheasants I shot
myself during a charity clays
tournament and had stuffed.

it is for fifty. Giving me the space for that was a major part of the initial renovation of the house.

The biggest and most costly challenge was moving the original fireplace, which sat against a wall smack-dab in the middle of the current space, ruining the sight lines I envisioned and just generally cramping my style. Though it was a major structural undertaking, relocating it (and getting rid of the wall) more than doubled the span of the room—it stretched from the front of the house to the back, giving the space lots more natural light as well as garden views and allowing for the free flow of rooms in the house's greater layout, a quality so necessary to its graceful function. (My idea of a perfect abode is one you can walk around in circles in, where every room is connected and you can go into and out of each one multiple ways.)

What I ended up with was an enormous space—nearly 1800 square feet—that on first glance seems like it would be the opposite of cozy. It's a scenario that will be familiar to many people living in open-plan houses with those kinds of lofty rooms. The key to turning a capacious space like that into a welcoming cocoon is to divide and conquer. I started out by splitting up the room into imaginary quadrants and gave each zone at least one, if not two, seating arrangements to anchor them. In order for this to work, each area has to have the requisites for comfort and function: sofas, chairs, settees, and ottomans, of course, but also plenty of surfaces within arm's length to set down a drink, adequate lighting for reading or conversing, and room for the aforementioned versatility, which is essential for seamless entertaining. Translation? In any given grouping, you should be able to pull up a garden stool, turn around a chair, or even move an occasional or games table to accommodate someone joining or leaving a clique at a bigger party or facilitating an activity like playing cards during a more intimate gathering. For me, aside from the sofas, no furniture configuration is set in stone—and that's only because I can't easily move a sofa at a moment's notice!

For a cocktail party, at least two-thirds of your guests should be able to find a seat. Believe it or not, in the living room there are indeed spots for thirty people to take a load off. But you'd never know it. The separate seating arrangements successfully split up the interior and tame its outsize proportions. That kind of malleability is perfect for entertaining and ideal for the rhythm of my life, embracing anyone who walks in the door, no matter how many people are coming over for dinner.

PREVIOUS PAGES: Wiley, my son's Labrador retriever, lounges on one of the sofas. The pedimented Georgian bookcases give height to a room with low seating. OPPOSITE AND ABOVE: Separate seating arrangements make a large space feel cozy. It helps if you can easily rearrange, too; I move the ottoman in front of the fire all the time to make room for a games or dining table.

(Gracious Living)
ECSTATIC ECLECTICISM

Now for the glamour part. Since I knew I'd have the right framework for the living room to function the way I wanted it to, I could have fun with the decoration. (Mental note: function is a great facilitator of whimsy, romance, and the truly personal. Since the underlying infrastructure ensures the space will run smoothly, it gives you the freedom to play with sensory variables like color, pattern, and texture.) Though its construction dates to the 1970s, the house is Georgian in spirit and I wanted to create a layered, vaguely English look that felt collected over time. I did my best to channel Nancy Lancaster and dove right in.

The jumping-off point was one of my most prized possessions: an enormous antique Oushak rug with all my favorite colors in it that blanketed nearly the entire room and was one of the only things I got to salvage from my former house. As a rule, I try not to get too attached to things—that's one of *the* great lessons you learn from a divorce—but this baby is something I'd try to save in a fire. It's an exotic woven garden of rich Prussian blues and warm terra-cottas, cinnabars, and ochers—the hues of earth, sky, and water. Nearly all the colors in the room, from the ikat stripe on the walls to the lacquer on the chinoiserie mirror to the velvets on the sofas and the tapestry pattern on one of the throw pillows, contain variations on those basic tones. Not exact matches, mind you, but riffs on the theme.

If you follow that general-color-family rule of thumb, the more you add to the mix—ikat, animal, chinoiserie, and small-scale prints; nineteenth-century famille rose export porcelain; contemporary and vintage art; Louis XV-, XVI-, and Georgian-style armchairs, settees, and bookcases; patent leather; velvet-covered sofas trimmed in grosgrain and dripping bullion fringe; a mother of pearl–clad cocktail table—the more it gets along together. Seriously. The effect is of a swirl of influences that, taken as a whole, is wonderfully forgiving and a showcase entirely your own.

Adding more life to that mix are furnishings in a range of elevations—low stools, ottomans, and cocktail tables; mid-height armchairs, side tables, and lamps; tall eighteenth-century Georgian bookcases and a chinoiserie secretary—that keep the atmosphere from becoming static. (A room in which every piece of furniture and accessory is the same height will go over like a lead balloon.) Ditto that for the bottom half of furniture. There should be an equitable mix of legs and skirts—bare legs on armchairs and tables, skirts on sofas, solid stools—so your eye gets a mix of impeded and uninterrupted views.

Forget about making everything match—interiors that feel collected are about finding a point of view and then reveling in it. No matter how wide-reaching your eye, seemingly disparate things will have a rapport, like eighteenth-century porcelain and a blue-and-white cachepot or an inlaid chinoiserie tray that echoes the hues of a leopard-print velvet.

(*Stylish Entertaining*)
A FIRESIDE CHRISTMAS DINNER

I get so excited for Christmas, I'm practically planning by July. Basically, I begin decorating for it the moment people put their forks down at Thanksgiving. I'm especially crazy about the tree, and the last thing I want it to be is ordinary. To achieve that, on top of the standard globe ornaments (in a mix of colors to match the living room in matte and shiny finishes), I layer in natural elements that I've spruced up myself. Essentially, I use spray adhesive to coat anything that will sit still in glitter: palm fronds, pine cones, bird nests, branches. Then I weave them into the tree itself, along with ribbon and tinsel and plain white lights.

It becomes a great backdrop for holiday parties—the wall-to-wall-people ones and the more intimate ones, the latter of which I like the most. The holidays often feel like an endless merry-go-round of nonstop festivities, so it can be a treat to have just a few close friends for dinner. Given the choice, I'll choose that over a crowd any day, which is precisely what I did.

I've said it before, but I like to move my parties around, even if I'm serving dinner. My guest list was only eight people deep, and hosting them in the dining room felt a little too formal. Besides, this was my tight-knit inner circle, so something cozier was in order. I moved the round ottoman from in front of the fireplace in the living room and put a sixty-inch circular table in its place. The table setting itself was toned down, at least by my standards: a beautifully hand-embroidered linen tablecloth to match the vintage Mottahedeh Sacred Bird & Butterfly china pattern, which I love because it truly goes with everything, and a glamorous arrangement of roses and greens in a silver punch bowl for the centerpiece.

For a group that small, it's easy to mix up whatever anyone wants in terms of a cocktail, but it's also fun to have something special on hand for the occasion. I used to love cherry cordials at Christmas as a kid and who didn't? I invented a chocolate cherry bourbon cocktail to try and capture that taste. I pulled together all the ingredients on a silver tray on the card table: bourbon, Luxardo maraschino cherries, and chocolate bitters (you mix two ounces of bourbon with a half ounce of cherry syrup and a dash of bitters over ice in each glass, then garnish with a cherry and a piece of chocolate). Cocktails are a great vehicle for capturing the nostalgia of the season in a whole new way and kick off the night just right.

To give the tree dimension, I start with standard globe ornaments in shades that match tones in the living room and then layer on branches, palm fronds, and pine cones that I coat in glitter and loads of real silver lead tinsel and lush velvet or satin ribbon.

RIGHT AND FOLLOWING PAGES:
With lots of flexible seating
arrangements, the big living
room easily accommodates
a sixty-inch round folding
table I keep on hand for
intimate dinners like a
fireside Christmas supper.
China I use year-round
adapts to holiday themes
with the addition of
plaid napkin rings and mini
poinsettias that prop up
place cards. To start, I
served chocolate cherry
bourbon cocktails.

I invented chocolate cherry bourbon cocktails to approximate the taste of cherry cordials, which I loved when I was a kid. Along with the drink itself, I passed around dishes of good dark chocolate for guests to nibble on while they sipped. The pairing was a smash hit.

Joie de Vivre

 **A**s the rest of this book makes pretty clear, I'm from the life-is-a-moveable-feast school of entertaining. What I mean is, I don't always host dinner parties in my dining room, and I will just as often set up shop in the library, the family room, or the pool cabana. (I've even contemplated hosting a party in the garage for a big birthday party. Seriously. But my garage is painted navy and it is *that* pretty!) Breaking out of the standard protocol tends to be more interesting for me—and especially for my guests. But even I admit there is a certain kind of magic to hosting people in a room tailor-made for eating, even if it's just replating takeout onto your favorite china, because you can art direct the variables: the flicker of candlelight, the gleam of crystal and silver, fireworks of pattern on porcelain and linens.

At the end of the day, creating atmosphere is what it's all about. One of the reasons I love entertaining at home so much is that you get to build a kind of cocoon. We're assaulted all day long by things that demand our attention. But when you have people over, there are no crowds for them to jostle through. No struggle to get the waiter's attention. There's no one coming over to tell you the name of the cow you're eating, or what plot of land the cherry tomatoes came from or whatever. You get real quality time with your friends. It's a chance to reconnect. People loosen up. Nobody's rushing off. They'll have one more cocktail. And they aren't on their phones, either; they're not sitting there scrolling Pinterest or Instagram. And that's exactly what design should do: put you in the moment, and make you feel as if there's nowhere else in the world you'd rather be.

When I first bought the house, the dining room lacked the panache I wanted it to have: mingy windows that didn't fit into the larger

OPPOSITE: A springtime arrangement of poppies and tulips riffs on the tones in the dining room, which also happen to coordinate with most of my china, giving me great freedom to mix and match. ABOVE: An antique sideboard provides a perch for nibbles and drinks and drawers for extra storage space. FOLLOWING PAGES: Multiple small arrangements, like roses and basil in mint julep cups, are a sweet alternative to statement centerpieces. Lacquered cantaloupe ceilings help cast a flattering glow under candlelight; the velvet screen blocks views to the butler's pantry without inhibiting the movement of servers (usually me!). PAGES 68-69: The chinoiserie wallpaper is based on a historic English design I commissioned from de Gournay.

architectural sensibility I was going for and a bad connection to service areas that I was revamping anyway (more on that later). Once I moved the doorway so it would better facilitate movement between the (renovated) kitchen and prep areas and solved the window problem with floor-to-ceiling, double-hung sashes, I pretty much had the blank slate I needed.

"Blank slate" is the key phrase here. Before my divorce, I lived, essentially, in an architectural landmark—a rambling and pristine 1920s Georgian-style house designed by Philip Trammell Shutze, one of Atlanta's most famous architects. His residential work is sought after by those in the know as *the* last word in the domestic ideal. And I loved it. Until I didn't. ("Be careful what you wish for" is one of life's great lessons.) Since the architecture itself was so significant, I had to be reverent with it, and understandably so. But it had such dominance over everything in the house; it was a force to be reckoned with. It began to feel like I was living in a museum—or worse, a mausoleum. When I was searching for my new house, I wanted none of that. What I craved was just a frame—a kind of glorified box, really—in which I could do whatever I wanted. I would make my mark with decoration: fabrics and furnishings and wallpapers and objects that meant something to me instead of "status" architecture.

So the blank slate of a dining room came as a relief. The most prominent design feature I chose was a series of chinoiserie wallpaper panels based on a historic English design that I commissioned from de Gournay in custom hues. The panels establish the room's color scheme with shades of cantaloupe, eggplant, and spinach. (Notice a theme?) But what they were *really* doing is showcasing the hues in the china I already owned, so that no matter which patterns I set the table with—and it's normally a mix of different ones—it would always look good. The rest of the room follows suit, with more spinach and cantaloupe tones splashed on the walls and ceiling and an added flourish of eggplant on the baseboards. I dressed the windows in pelmets and curtains that I was able to bring from my last house. They're made from a printed Fortuny damask that happened to coordinate well. They were too bright at first, but laying them out for a couple of days in the Georgia sun solved *that* problem. Side note: Not everything has to be perfect. Second side note: Vintage curtains are a wonderful secret weapon, even if you only intend to repurpose them as a tablecloth or vanity skirt. Fabric is expensive and good custom curtains doubly so, but second-hand versions can be had for a song at estate sales and charity shops.

PREVIOUS PAGES: Peak-season fruit is just as good for centerpieces as flowers. ABOVE: Reflective surfaces, like a neoclassical mirror and mirrored sconces, are magical in dining rooms, because they extend the sparkle. OPPOSITE: All the furnishings in the room use the same tones of spinach, cantaloupe, and eggplant so they coexist well together.

The other hero piece in the room is a gorgeous and massive George III breakfront with its original oval glass panels that I bought at auction. News flash: people say no one wants "brown" antique furniture these days, which is just fine by me because it means fabulous pieces like this are wildly accessible. I'm not joking—I paid less for it than I would for an off-the-shelf cabinet, except this one features book-matched, heavily figured mahogany you can't buy new anywhere anymore, elegant neoclassical lines that will never go out of style, and the kind of craftsmanship that's already lasted a couple hundred years. Eventually, the rage for everything industrial will wane, people will want old things made with integrity again, and I'll be sitting on a gold mine—though that's not the reason I bought it at all. Beauty needs no excuse, does it?

An antique sideboard across the room completes the English country vibe and has a serpentine front that echoes the shape of the pelmets. It's got beaucoup storage (I put all my extra light bulbs in the drawers), so it's functional and gives me a place to serve buffet style. Just so the mood doesn't get too stuffy, I made sure to bring in plenty of sparkle. We've got twinkle in spades: a vintage crystal chandelier, antique sconces, a high-gloss lacquered ceiling, and a tall, gilded neoclassical mirror that acts almost like another window, except it magnifies all the candlelight, china, crystal, and animated faces interacting over the table. What can I say? It *is* pure magic.

For me, a swirl of patterns—ikats, birds, botanicals, geometrics—is always more interesting for a table than a matching suite of place settings. Etched water and white wineglasses add another layer of dimension.

THE ART OF SETTING THE TABLE

Let's start with the table itself. Mine's an old farmhouse-y version my mother gave me that wouldn't necessarily fit in with the rest of the things in the dining room, but I liked its oval shape. For my purposes, the way it looks is beside the point, because I would be covering it with a tablecloth. I'm a huge proponent of tablecloths. In one fell swoop, they let you change the entire look of the room: starched white hemstitched linens raise the formality stakes, while a print or pattern—animal, ikat, stripe, or otherwise—can take it in any number of different directions. I change my cloth seasonally (a lemon-yellow zebra stripe in summer, a printed damask that's much like the curtains in the fall).

I take a similar approach with the chairs, lovely vintage Louis XVI–style versions that I bought at Scott Antique Markets, a semi-regular show housed in two airplane hangars that's an Atlanta institution. I covered the cushions in a plush silk velvet that's very versatile, but I have slipcovers in my arsenal, too: cute apple-green gingham, heavy white cotton duck with scalloped edges, tailored duchesse silk in my signature shade of Prussian blue. Like the tablecloths, they change the entire personality of the room.

Now for the fun part: china. When clients ask for advice, I tell them to choose ten different colors they like and then look for at least four *different* patterns that feature those colors. If they're buying service for twelve, then they build it from those four different patterns: four place settings from one, four from the next, and so on. It gives you the ability for tons of variation, mixing and matching from the different patterns to create something truly all your own. It also means that if you have repeat guests, they're less likely to see the same table twice. You can scale up this method to encompass larger collections; I had one client who bought twelve different sets of service for twelve, all within the same color family. That's 144 different possible combinations!

Which brings me to my next piece of advice. So long as you're working within the same family of hues—that's the largest takeaway here—don't sweat the matching part. It'll go together, I promise. And the more you add to the mix, the more forgiving—and unique—the scheme. Think like a collector and build up a stockpile with the same general philosophy: napkins, napkin rings, flatware, glassware, platters, trays, saltcellars, place mats, candlesticks, etc. When you go to set the table, you'll be drawing on a palette just like a painter, with a little of this and a little of that, composing a one-night-only masterpiece your guests will swoon over.

Collect china with patterns in the same basic color families and you'll be able to mix and match at will, combining different sets with abandon to land on something all your own.

Let's Get Cooking

Architecturally speaking, the kitchen is the house's outlier because my inspiration wasn't Georgian in origin, it was classic Americana. On the outside, the structure—part of a new wing that includes the mud hall and garage—fits in with the house's overall profile, but from the inside it resembles nothing so much as a big lofty barn. The ceilings soar overhead, and the airy space is soaked in natural light from southern-facing windows and two tall French doors. It's big enough to encompass everything I need, which are requisites for kitchens, as far as I'm concerned: plenty of storage for both food and tools, multiple workstations organized by function, a tall hood for ample ventilation (cooking smells should stay in the kitchen), and task-specific lighting.

To be clear, large doesn't necessarily always mean efficient. My last kitchen was enormous, but also enormously *inefficient*. I felt like I was constantly running around the island. You have to pay close attention to function. A good rule of thumb is the classic kitchen triangle theory—that the trajectory between fridge, sink, and cooktop should form a loose triangle to facilitate storage, prep, and cooking. In my case, the space allowed me to have two triangles organized around two sinks: one around the range and fridge for cooking, and the other around the pantry and ovens for baking. A dishwasher and hidden storage for trash at both sinks mean the setup is supremely practical: just slice, toss, and load at each station and you won't feel like you've run a marathon to get dinner on the table. The division also allowed me to separate my prep and cooking cleanup from my post-meal cleanup. One dishwasher gets pots and pans, the other gets crystal and china. (Mix them in the same loads and you end up with

ABOVE: Two sinks—one near the stove for cooking and the other near the ovens for baking—mean I don't have to run circles around the kitchen when I'm entertaining. OPPOSITE: Storage is supremely task-specific, with compartments that slide out for easy access; no digging into dark cubbies for me. FOLLOWING PAGES: The kitchen is part of the new wing I added during the renovation, with soaring proportions and a crisp blue-and-white scheme; the counters are gray marble in a leathered finish, so they feel soft and don't look too shiny.

Kitchen organization is the number one requisite for stress-free entertaining. If you have to rummage around dark cabinets to find anything, you're working too hard.

fleabites on the china. And yes, I *do* wash my good stuff in the dishwasher. "Fine" china is an oxymoron because it implies delicacy, but porcelain is pretty durable.)

The island is big enough for dining, and at first that was a big point of contention for me. Call me old-fashioned, but in the past I've felt like meals at the counter are way too loosey-goosey. In practice, however, the ample island has been a revelation. It gives people a comfortable place to park and keep me company while I'm cooking and—proof that people can change—I've discovered that sometimes I actually *like* an easier, more casual meal at the counter. With teenagers in the house, it's become especially useful. They gravitate to eating at the counter as if pulled by a magnet. I'm forever being called into service late at night to cook up grilled cheeses, and if that sounds like a complaint, I assure you it's not. Consider me a dining-counter convert.

When it comes to storage, I'm as fanatical about organization in the kitchen as I am everywhere else, with the same basic philosophy: if you can't see it and easily access it, you can't use it (and cooking for a dinner party will send you over the edge). There are specific drawers for spices, knives, and utensils, plus cabinets with shelves that slide out or pop up so I'm not digging into dark spaces for pots, cleaning supplies, or minor appliances. The cabinet where I keep things like the blender and food processor is equipped with electrical outlets, so I don't have to lug them too far to use them. Sheet pans are stored vertically in slots arranged by size behind cabinet doors. In all the houses I've lived in and with all the entertaining I've done, I've *never* had enough fridge or freezer space, so in this place I installed two refrigerators and one freezer.

ABOVE: To me, it's just not a kitchen without a screen door.
OPPOSITE AND FOLLOWING PAGES: Open shelves, porcelain, and crockery keep frequently used items close at hand. Encaustic French bistro tiles are laid out in a nondirectional hexagonal pattern, look good from every direction, and are virtually indestructible.

To up the design game in the kitchen, disguise built-ins and appliances such as cabinetry and refrigerators behind furniture-esque details like cornices, baseboards, and nailhead trim.

Of course, this kitchen had to feel stylistically of a piece with the rest of the house. Most of the millwork is cloaked in my favorite shade of Prussian blue. I don't like the look of built-in cabinetry, so I made mine look like armoires or vitrines with decorative cornices and baseboards. The refrigerators and a pantry are hidden behind lacquered plywood doors that I outlined in nailhead trim; they look like a million bucks. Drawer and cabinet pulls are a mix of vintage department-store door handles I scored at an estate sale and off-the-shelf brass hardware inspired by ship interiors. They don't match, and I didn't want them to—matchy-matchy environments give me the heebie-jeebies. (Perfection is impossible, so why make it the goal?) I wallpapered the backs of glass-fronted cabinets, which hold easy-to-get-at snacks on one side and baking basics on the other, in the same pattern I used on the walls in the butler's pantry for a thread throughout that adds cohesion.

The floors are covered in encaustic tiles laid in a mosaic pattern of hexagons bordered by a Greek-key motif that everyone and their mother tried to talk me out of: I'd get tired of the pattern, it would affect resale value, they'd look dirty. Well, I trusted my instincts and I'm glad I did. The tiles are indestructible, which comes in handy in a kitchen, and to me, the pattern feels like a neutral. It's basically a rug I get to have in a space in which you'd never put one. My greatest stroke of genius vis-à-vis the floors, however, has nothing to do with the way they look, but the way they feel. They're heated, so when I walk in there on a frosty winter morning to get my coffee and toast, it's like walking on warm sand.

OPPOSITE: I papered the back of cabinets with the same Brunschwig & Fils Le Touche pattern I used on the walls in the butler's pantry and on portieres for the china cabinet. ABOVE: The brass shelf brackets are brass plated upside-down sneeze-guard frames. What can I say? Inspiration hit me one day at the salad bar.

(*Stylish Entertaining*)
A FRIED-CHICKEN BUFFET SUPPER IN THE KITCHEN

I used to be dead set against entertaining at the kitchen counter because I thought it was way too casual a venue to imbue a proper sense of occasion. But the advent of my kids turning into teenagers—for whom casual is a raison d'être—and the fact that the actual cooking of the meal can be part of the entertainment, especially when the group is close friends and family, has made me a convert.

One of my favorite things to do at the kitchen counter is host a fried-chicken supper buffet. Since fried chicken is best when it's hot from the pan, it requires you to be active right up until the point you're ready to serve. With a party in the kitchen, though, that becomes part of the fun. I'll prepare everything but the chicken in advance and set up a buffet on the counter by the window, so when guests arrive, I can just warm up the frying pan and get to work. They'll pour themselves a drink from a pitcher I've mixed up (and they'll pour me one, too), mingle around the counter, and keep me company while I finish up dinner. It is charming and festive and doesn't feel like even a lick of work.

MENU

Mixed Green Salad
Classic Potato Salad
Southern Baked Beans
Cornbread Muffins
Buttermilk Fried Chicken
Grapefruit Spritzers

OPPOSITE AND FOLLOWING PAGES: I used to hate dining at the kitchen counter—and then I had teenagers. Now it's a place where I actually entertain guests, especially when something that needs to be prepared à la minute, like fried chicken, is on the menu, because the party can join me while I cook.

Breakfast of Champions

 onventional wisdom these days says that dining rooms—purpose-driven spaces in which you only eat—are a thing of the past. Obviously, I'm not a proponent of *that* particular school of thought, and my dining room isn't the kind of encased-in-amber zone that theory looks to avoid anyway, but I already had one formal dining room in the house. As much as I love to entertain, even *I* didn't need another. The breakfast room, situated off a hallway that connects to the kitchen, is a different kind of venue; meant to feel casual and unbuttoned, it's more like a sunroom or an indoor porch. It's made for eating in, yes, but it can just as easily accommodate a business meeting and is way more inviting than a standard-issue conference room. With French doors on two sides and sunlight flooding through the windows, it's as close as I could get to being in the garden without actually moving outside. The pergola in the *potager* is just steps beyond the glass doors. You can sit in there and watch the zinnias bobbing in the breeze and hummingbirds flitting from bloom to bloom. In the winter, on those rare Atlanta days when everything is blanketed in snow, it's like being in the thick of it—without even having to put a sweater on.

In such an exposed space, the relationship between what's inside and what's outside is key to making it work. I didn't want the interiors to compete with the profusion of foliage and blossoms on view for much of the year. Banana palms in blue-and-white pots provided the tiniest touch of green—just enough to create a connection. Placed on stands, they're also extremely tall, drawing the eye upward and emphasizing ceiling heights. Since the flowers that bloom in the part of the garden visible from the windows tend

OPPOSITE: A wicker chest and woven water-hyacinth armchairs achieve a delicate high-low balance with a Georgian mirror in a gesso finish and parrots on brackets once owned by Sister Parish. ABOVE: Blue-and-gray cork floors in a classic rhombille pattern line the hallway between the kitchen and breakfast room, bridging the spaces in an unexpected way. FOLLOWING PAGES: Purely decorative curtains hung in the corners of the room add a sense of cushy softness and draw the eye up, along with tall banana palms in blue-and-white planters.

A generous double exposure is the main event in the sun-drenched breakfast room, which makes you feel like you're in the thick of the garden—and you don't even have to put on your shoes.

to be in warm red and orange tones, I painted the room blue, although I never need much of an excuse to use a variation on my signature shade. Pinch-pleated blue-and-white curtains hung from the ceiling at the corners of the room are purely decorative—why have a sunroom in which you block out the sun?—but it's the kind of decorative touch that's necessary. They add a lush layer of softness to the room, creating a hushed atmosphere that recalls the living room's ikat walls with added tactile dimension. The floors, like those on classic porches everywhere, are painted white.

Furnishings are elegant but laid-back, with a high-low mix I like to think of as "chinoiserie veranda." A vintage wicker chest (the low part of the equation) is crowned by a Georgian mirror (the high) that's gorgeously subdued thanks to its original gesso finish. It's flanked by sculptural birds on brackets once owned by Sister Parish that also have a creamy finish and are among my most prized possessions. There's a painted-tole pagoda lantern above the table in the place of a chandelier, mining that indoor-outdoor vibe again, and the table itself is vintage McGuire rattan paired with big comfy armchairs woven from thick, ribbed braids of water hyacinth—a dramatic flourish of texture that brings the whole scene right down to earth.

ABOVE AND OPPOSITE: Royal Copenhagen china and a Wedgwood basalt centerpiece feel like they were basically made for the breakfast room, which I use a lot for its intended purpose, especially when guests are staying. It's also brilliant for business meetings or casual lunches—the light is just divine.

FOURTH OF JULY
ON THE KITCHEN PATIO

Since most of the garden is pretty formal and structured, the kitchen patio is the area I designated for experimenting. I try out different colors and blooms, and things get a little interesting and wild. I put in rosebushes and climbing hydrangeas, pretty little Japanese maples and red honeysuckles. In the summer, it's like a bird sanctuary, with hummingbirds galore. I delineated the area from the *potager*, which it borders, with lattice so it has an old-fashioned (in a good way!) garden-club feel. It also has direct access to the kitchen through tall screen doors, another old-fashioned thing I *had* to have. I grew up with them, and to me, it's not summer without the sound of the screen door slamming.

The patio feels like an extension of the kitchen, which is great for me, as I'm from Texas, and I needed a place to barbecue! It's an outdoor dining area with a casual picnic-in-the-park feel, furnished with wrought-iron armchairs and a sofa outfitted with cushions in a simple blue and white–striped fabric, for which I have matching tablecloths. When July rolls around, it is always the perfect spot for a Fourth of July cookout for a few friends.

With the right approach, you can give even hot dogs and hamburgers a sense of occasion, and that's exactly what I did here. Gerbera daisies and geraniums provided the tablescape with firework-red tones and I couldn't resist adding small American flags to a basket of hydrangeas. When I'm building a table outdoors the wind can sometimes be a problem, so I have a whole arsenal of heavy accessories that won't fly away in a breeze. My favorites are chargers made from slats of wood that give the scene a rustic feel. I matched them with wicker-wrapped water glasses and simple wine goblets. Nickel-rimmed hurricane lanterns and blue-enameled flatware added just the right touch of elegance. And so the whole thing didn't veer too far into seen-it-all-before territory, I chose napkins in a red, green, and navy plaid—a slightly off-kilter choice. I can't help it—the matchy-matchy game is not my thing.

OPPOSITE AND FOLLOWING PAGES: The kitchen patio is equipped with a barbecue and is a barefoot-casual part of the garden—a perfect venue, in other words, for a Fourth of July supper featuring hot dogs and hamburgers and nary a paper plate in sight.

The Party Pantry

Even though this feels a little like admitting to a serious hoarding tendency, the china pantry, a.k.a. the party pantry, is quite possibly my favorite spot in the entire house. It's honestly my dream come true: an unfussy, utilitarian space in which all that I could ever need for entertaining is stored. It's one-stop access for all my candles, crystal, china, linens, vases, baskets, trays, napkins, glassware, flatware, you name it. Most of the stuff is organized by set or color on open shelving or hanging racks, while flatware, place mats, and napkins are organized by sets in drawers, so I can see it all in one fell swoop and build a table just by walking in the room, picking and choosing elements as I go.

My thinking is that if you see it, you use it—we all know how things tucked away behind doors or in closets just end up collecting dust. Everything should have a place, and if it goes back in the same place, you always know where it is and when you need to repair it, replace it, or stock up. Running a house is pretty much about mastering supply-chain management. I'm fairly certain I was a great military logistician in a past life, because I'm very systems-oriented.

Quite simply, that kind of organization makes having people over for a party or dinner feel effortless. It's also the secret to setting really inventive tables. You're able to mix and match with abandon because you're working with a full painter's palette, so to speak. You're also more likely to use finer objects, such as the wedding china you normally reserve for special occasions—a practice I'm not a big fan of. Why shouldn't you drink your morning coffee or eat your oatmeal out of bone china? Don't you deserve it? And honestly, when else are you going to use it? On the once-every-leap-year time you decide to host a formal breakfast? Who

ABOVE: Portieres instead of doors mean I don't have to fuss with doorknobs when I'm carrying a stack of glassware or china. When I want to hide the closet, they seamlessly draw closed. OPPOSITE AND FOLLOWING PAGES: The china pantry is quite possibly my favorite space in the house; since I can see every entertaining staple I own on open shelves, it makes setting the table easy, effortless, and inventive.

When you can see practically your entire entertaining arsenal in one fell swoop, inventive, unexpected, and personal tablescapes feel effortless and are also a whole lot of fun.

are we kidding? Using so-called special accessories in a regular way does two things: it honors precious items by employing them the way they were intended and elevates an experience that might otherwise feel banal—just try it with tomorrow's coffee and see. It also makes for enchanting and surprising juxtapositions: I'll readily mix something plainspoken like stoneware or charming majolica with painted porcelain. The high-low combination can be magical.

Just outside the pantry is a butler's prep area connecting the kitchen on one side to the dining room on the other. It's equipped with an ice maker, wine and drink fridges, and a deep sink. When I'm entertaining formally, I'll block off the view to the hallway from the dining room with a folding screen. But whenever it's a really large group, like at the holidays, it becomes the buffet area where I set out serving dishes so people can come and go at their own pace. The walls are covered in a blue-and-white wallpaper that matches the portieres I can draw shut to close off the china pantry—who wants to fuss with doors when you're walking in and out with glassware and china? The color palette helps to bridge the dining room and kitchen and feels cohesive with the china pantry.

When the kids are all home and we're having dinner, setting the table is one of their chosen tasks. I always tell them there are no rules to it, and it's brilliant because I can hear them in the china pantry going "Hmm," as they mull over different combinations, matching their choices to whatever we're eating, the time of year, or the way they feel. Suddenly a simple, normally throwaway act—setting the table for supper—becomes something more. A cabbage-leaf bowl or a transferware plate transforms into a vehicle for creativity, for being present, for being together, for *joy*. And bingo! *That's* what good design can do.

ABOVE: To accentuate vintage Tabasco ad prints by Ludwig Bemelmans, I matted them with extra bits of Le Touche wallpaper. OPPOSITE: Right outside the china pantry is a prep area I use like a butler's pantry. That's Maybelline, our standard poodle, waiting for her four o'clock treat! FOLLOWING PAGES: Everything in the pantry is organized by pattern, color, or type.

106

All in the Family

've never been the kind of mother who made certain rooms off-limits to my kids, no matter what age they were. My thinking has always been to teach them how to behave in a variety of settings, from casual to formal, and let the milk, juice, or Coca-Cola fall where it may. If you expose children to quality art and antiques early on and show them how to respect those objects, and accept the occasional accident as just another ding or dent in a given piece's centuries-old history, then they will learn to appreciate those things in an intrinsic way that you can never later explain. The family room encapsulates that approach for me. Although my children are all young adults now and know how to use a coaster, I wanted the room to combine the refinement I've always tried to show them with a put-your-feet-up kind of ease that, thanks to their upbringing, I knew they'd appreciate.

The space is near the kitchen, close to the major action of mealtimes, and meant for watching TV, playing games like backgammon and gin rummy, reading, or just hanging out. It was part of the new addition I added to the house in the renovation, and to combat that fresh-laid-Sheetrock vibe, I wanted to give it a healthy sense of history. My mind went immediately to the idea of paneled walls, but I had to consider atmosphere. Though the room backs onto the garden, it only has one exposure, so it wasn't ever going to get a ton of natural light. Dark walnut or oak would have felt totally leaden. So I used cypress limed and glazed to a luminous gray hue that added gravitas and texture, thanks to boiserie-like carving and wood graining still visible through the glaze. To further play up that effect, I installed a bleached-wood pattern on the dark floor, which outlines the perimeter of the

OPPOSITE: Since the family room was part of the new addition, I installed limed and glazed cypress paneling to give it a sense of history; I also stripped and bleached the Georgian console table so it would fit in. ABOVE: Cool blue tones and washed-out grays mingle with warmer coral tones in the space to help enhance the natural light. FOLLOWING PAGES: I used Brunschwig & Fils's classic Le Lac fabric as a leitmotif on curtains, pillows, and armchairs; repeating a single fabric like this can help pull a room together.

111

room with a Greek-key motif and frames the rug—a room-sized remnant I had cut down from a ginormous granny-chic needlepoint pattern designed by Mario Buatta that I bought at an estate sale.

The idea of cutting down a rug to suit my situation goes right to my point. Nothing should ever be too precious to adapt to your lifestyle—whether that includes kids, dogs, or your cousin Cheryl wobbling a glass of red wine. Do you own your possessions, or do your possessions own you?

Throughout this room I asked myself that question again and again, and I bet you can guess how I answered. There are the deep, English-y sofas covered in a Prussian-blue linen velvet that for some reason known only to them and God are the preferred lounging spots for wet Rollins dogs. (Linen velvet, by the way, is *such* a deceptive material because it feels so extravagant, but it's so hard-wearing as to be virtually indestructible.) A Georgian console table that I bought thinking I would use it as a desk had just the right sculptural lines—cabriole legs, ball-and-claw feet, egg-and-dart apron—to anchor a large piece of contemporary art against a wall. But *not* in its original dark finish, which would have had the entirely wrong attitude and put the whole room askew. So I had it stripped and bleached to match the walls. The juxtaposition, against a contemporary abstract piece, is to die for. And do you know what I do with the saucers that go along with the myriad porcelain teacups I don't often have the occasion to use? They're coasters for pots of geraniums or ferns dotted around the space.

I hung art with the same irreverence, sometimes letting the panels on the walls frame them, sometimes ignoring the panels completely so they hang right over the carved seams. It's an eclectic mix: actual pieces of eighteenth-century export porcelain interspersed with framed prints of the stuff by artist John Matthew Moore. I like the surprising switch from two to three dimensions. There is even room in here for objects almost no one but me would think of as art, like a sunflower blossom literally gone to seed that I think is beautiful in its complex simplicity and which reminds me of a certain period in my life. Do you see what I'm trying to say? I'm all for understanding the basic rules of design, but that doesn't mean I'm going to do something just because that's the way it's always been done. In our houses, meaning should be wherever *we* want to put it, whichever way *we* see fit. It's the only real way to actually ever possess anything.

PREVIOUS PAGES: Prints of blue-and-white export china by John Matthew Moore are interspersed with the real thing for an unexpected play on dimensions. OPPOSITE: Set up multiple entertaining stations like this throughout the house and you won't have to trek all over the place to offer someone a drink. ABOVE: It's always five o'clock somewhere!

PREVIOUS PAGES: Don't ignore the details. Fringe, tapes, pom-poms, Greek-key borders, and nailhead trim are the kind of touches that add up to a one-of-a-kind space. RIGHT: For some reason, Rollins dogs love the family room sofas, especially when they've come in from the yard soaking wet; it's a good thing linen velvet is virtually indestructible and manages to look luxe anyway. I've never been one to cordon off living areas from kids or pets.

(*Stylish Entertaining*)
VALENTINE'S DAY DINNER
IN THE FAMILY ROOM

The saying goes that April is the cruelest month, but I'd like to respectfully suggest that be amended to February, at least in the South. By April, everything down here is blooming and we've long since shed our heavy winter overcoats. There's no push and pull from warm to chill, no wildly variable weather to leave you high and dry (or cold and sopping wet, as it were).

February, on the other hand, is a mean little time of year. The festivities of the holidays are long behind us, the charm of new beginnings and resolutions is wearing thin, and everyone's dying for a little sunshine and heat. And that's before the specter of Valentine's Day rears its head. By the end of January, we're practically drowning in hearts and roses and drugstore samplers. It all feels a little too showy for me.

Which is why I was so excited to learn that my friend Lance would be in town when V-Day last rolled around. It was the perfect reason to host a little low-key dinner for him and a couple of other friends. I thought of it as the antidote to going out since it really is one of the most dreadfully contrived days of the year to go out to dinner, anyway. The family room was the perfect venue: it's unbuttoned and relaxed, the backgammon table is already set up by the fireplace, and the exotic theme going on in there would help me devise a table that used warm Valentine's Day colors in a completely unexpected way.

A suzani tablecloth with coral and magenta tones gave me permission to mix up porcelain in a range of geometric patterns, all in shades of raspberry. (It proves my theory that the more you mix in, the more you *can* mix in.) I used hefty silver flatware to slightly counteract the casual vibe I was going for, while ikat napkins brought the whole thing together. For the flowers, I made an arrangement of red anemones and ranunculus—a riff on the seasonal theme that feels as far away from cardboard-cutout hearts and paper lace as you can get. The meal itself was halfway homemade. I whipped up tomato bisque and chocolate pots de crème myself and used them to bracket restaurant rotisserie chicken with roasted green beans and carrots. Take that, Cupid!

The games table in the family room easily transforms into an entertaining venue that packs intimacy, atmosphere, and charm into one pretty package—all without having to move a single stick of furniture.

I've never been afraid of clashing anything in my entire life: a good formula for an unconventional table setting is to choose one color family and then layer in pattern on top of pattern on top of pattern.

Happy Hour

Tucked behind a jib door inset into the wallpapered wall of the living room is a space no inveterate entertainer should have to go without: their very own bar. I outfitted this surprise jewel box of a space with all the necessary accoutrements, from wine and beverage fridges to an ice maker, to create a festive little annex for the living room, which is where I probably entertain the most. I love that when people come over, I can pop open the door and pour them a drink without having to trek to the kitchen at the other end of the house. And it's also supremely useful during parties.

I echoed warmer cream and cinnabar shades from the living room rug on a diagonal chevron pattern I had painted on the floor. While it looks super fancy, I did the pattern myself with a ruler until I threw my back out and a friend, decorative painter Mary Meade Evans, came to my rescue. The bar itself is literally a modular shell designed to hide appliances that I could move if I had to, topped in brass with a cinnabar faux ostrich-leather bumper. I used a happy print for the tufted upholstery on the sides of the bar and to cover cabinet fronts, which, like the drawers and shelves, are literally cabinet-grade plywood made by my carpenter and painted. Two collections comprise the art: vintage hotel ashtrays I've, um, *collected* over the years and a series of framed vintage whiskey ads illustrated by Ludwig Bemelmans that depict a nouveau-riche Texan traveling the globe with his butler and are as charming as they sound. With Prussian blue walls the room was a bit on the chilly side, so I came up with the idea of a filigree molding. It looks like vintage Edwardian grillwork, but it's balsa wood decorative trim I spray painted a metallic brass shade. I also lined the cabinet fronts in brass chicken wire—a country French detail, courtesy of my local Home Depot.

ABOVE AND OPPOSITE: Despite a small footprint, the bar packs quite an impact thanks to a myriad of details. There's a full complement of glassware and accessories, velvet trim; a collection of vintage ashtrays hung like art; and a painted floor that reprises colors in the adjoining rooms. FOLLOWING PAGES: The tufted bar, covered in Schumacher's Citrus Garden fabric, is just a plywood shell my carpenter whip up.

126

Shelf Life

The library is a space I carved out of the house's former master bedroom, and it's like lounge city. Somebody's *always* in there. It connects to the living room through the bar on one side, so whomever it is will have gotten him- or herself something to drink—a soda, cocktail, or otherwise—and will be sitting in there, chatting or reading or staring at the fire. Of course that makes *me* super happy, because that's exactly what I designed it for. I think of it as a sweet riposte to the living room: where that room is a little grand and expansive, this is snug and easeful. The living room is a glamorous backdrop for a party, while this a warm setting for a heart-to-heart. It feels like a safe little escape away from it all, even though it's practically in the center of the house.

The room faces north, so it gets the kind of cool, diffuse light that can sometimes use a little warming up. Light is a huge factor in determining what kind of color a room can handle. A southern exposure with floods of intense sunlight, for example, probably calls for a cooler hue to take some of that heat off. Following my philosophy of carrying the same colors throughout the house, I riffed on the cinnabar tones in the living room and cloaked the walls and millwork in a toasty shade of orange.

To be honest, at first it looked like a huge traffic cone. But I'm never really afraid of going out on a limb with something like that. The worst-case scenario is that you paint again, and all *that* entails is a couple more gallons and a weekend. What I could see, despite how blaring the shade initially felt, was that the windows offered a view onto trees and shrubs and lawn that are gorgeous and green most of the year. I knew that highlighting those verdant surroundings would

ABOVE, OPPOSITE, AND FOLLOWING PAGES: A midcentury-modern bronze, brass, and glass desk by Bernhard Rohne and a wicker table designed by Dorothy Draper for the Carlyle Hotel are an unexpected but winning combination; collect what you love and your spaces will begin to have a logic all their own.

Everyone from pets to people gravitate to the library and it's no surprise—it's the coziest, comfiest, most away-from-it-all spot in the house.

soften the orange's glaring effect. So to fully tame it and ground the entire room, I covered the walls themselves in Prussian blue grass cloth, leaving just the millwork orange as a kind of exclamation point. The texture and the tone on the walls help to draw the foliage indoors—the grass cloth's ribbing is almost like tree bark, and the blue shade captures the backdrop of sky—and they're a striking counterpoint to the rich glow of orange.

Everything else in the room channels that kind of push-and-pull tension: plump armchairs and a deep sofa in mottled, watery prints by Lisa Fine Textiles juxtaposed against an antique rug in smoldering tones that mirrors the exotic flavor of the fabrics; French 1940s still lifes of flowers and fruit and a contemporary abstract work by Michael Quinn decommissioned from Atlanta's High Museum of Art that combines their hues and looks as if they've been fused and abstracted; a sharp, midcentury brass, bronze, and glass desk by Bernhard Rohne and a wicker table that Dorothy Draper designed for the Carlyle Hotel in New York City; and a masculine dark-metal Empire chandelier and flamboyant gilded chinoiserie mirror that I painted white.

If you took inventory of all these things and looked at them on paper, they'd seem like the stream-of-consciousness ravings of a misguided design geek. They shouldn't work. But they do, and it's precisely because they're so specific. They reflect the point of view of one particular design lover—me. I'm not saying I'm a savant, either, but here's the secret: If you collect things that speak to you, they start to have a logic all their own and they will always find themselves a place inside your home.

PREVIOUS PAGES: The gilding on a Georgian mirror felt too glitzy, so I painted it matte white. Books, a fireplace, cushy seating: is it any wonder the library is a go-to for a cozy catch-up over an old-fashioned? ABOVE AND OPPOSITE: French 1940s still lifes play up the tones in the marine blue grass cloth on the walls, which I chose for its texture and the way it tamed the warm citrus millwork.

136

(*Stylish Entertaining*)
ALWAYS READY FOR FRIENDS

Considering how much I love to entertain, it's probably not all that surprising that I have one of those houses: it sits on a prominent corner of a well-traveled street, and people I know are always driving by. It's not at all unusual for a friend to be cruising along, see my car out front or smoke billowing from the chimney, and pull off the road to say hi.

Since I work from home and everyone knows I've got a pretty liberal open-door policy, I try to keep stocked with enough staples to make unexpected guests feel like I'm psychic. I do this for a lot of reasons, but chief among them is that I am a firm believer that catching up over a cocktail or a cup of tea by the fire in the library is always going to be better than meeting someone at a crowded bar or random Starbucks. Also, I love having the kind of house that people feel they can just pop into. Being prepared is the best way to make that happen. (And when I *am* in the middle of something, such as busy with work or otherwise preoccupied, no one's ever offended if I beg off and send them away with a peck on the cheek and an "I'll call you later.")

Here's my list of pantry and fridge staples that I always keep stocked so no one ever catches me off guard:

- Assorted teas and tisanes
- Bourbon
- Tequila
- Gin
- Vodka
- Tonic and sparkling water
- Lemons, limes, and oranges for tea or cocktails
- Hard cheeses with a long shelf life, like Parmesan and aged Gouda
- Cherry preserves to serve with cheese
- Assorted crackers
- Packaged cheese straws
- High-quality potato chips
- Crème frâiche
- Caviar
- Assorted nuts, but especially pistachios (they're fun to eat)
- Dried fruit like figs and Turkish apricots
- Dark chocolate

Keep your pantry stocked with a smorgasbord of nibbles that have a long shelf life. Not only will you never go hungry, you'll also always be prepared to host unexpected guests for tea, coffee, or a cocktail.

Powder Compact

Just between the library and the living room is the powder room, which functions as the main restroom at my parties. As I've said before, I like to imagine the actual *life* a space will lead. So when you are at a party and you want to reapply your lipstick or powder your nose, you'll need somewhere to sit and a glamorous mirror to look into. And then someone else will need to come in and tell you what so-and-so just did or said (as far as I'm concerned, it's not a party if there's not something powder room–worthy to talk about), and so *she'll* need a place to sit, and then maybe your other friend will come in too, and she (or he!) *actually* has to use the bathroom….

Imagine a modernized, mini version of a fancy French restaurant bathroom from the 1940s—the kind of place where Joan Crawford would smooth out her updo. There's a separate water closet with a door for privacy, but also a sitting area with a vanity skirted in silk taffeta overflowing with ruffles and pleats and a Regency mirror dripping with gilt fronds and pagodas. There's a plump Louis XVI settee for gossiping on, sconces and lamps outfitted with silk shades, and, to keep things sophisticated, a chinoiserie wallpaper with birds and blooms from Fromental. On the walls I've hung fabulous, Erté-esque illustrations painted by Miles Redd, my former decorator, mentor, and dear friend. Sentimental and stylish is one of my favorite combinations, and it helped me achieve a powder room that's more than the sum of its parts. What they say about dressing for the life you want to lead is true in decoration, too: design a room for the life you want to have and see if it doesn't come true.

OPPOSITE: A silk taffeta table skirt actually disguises the extra storage for breath mints, powder puffs, makeup wipes, aspirin, and the like that I put in the powder room for guests. ABOVE: A Louis XVI settee provides extra seating in the space, the main restroom for guests at parties. It's so boring to go to the powder room alone; the Erté-like illustrations are by Miles Redd.

Master Class

When it came time to design the master suite—an architectural addition just off the living room that added another wing to the house and enclosed the back garden—I sat down and thought really hard about how I wanted to use the space. I knew I'd be asking a lot from it. I'm a creative person working in a creative field who doesn't do well in traditional office settings, an introverted extrovert who needs quite a bit of time alone, a single woman in her fifties with a desire for a personal sanctuary, and an inveterate entertainer who thrives on having people over and feting them in unexpected places. (And yes, I realize some of those concepts contradict one another. Now do you see why design can be so complicated?)

In other words, this couldn't be a place just for sleeping. Practically speaking, the wing had to function as a self-contained live-work space that would bend easily to a variety of uses—as a command center, home office, and party venue for intimate friends—yet still hold its own as a place of refuge where I could retreat when I need a little downtime.

The concept I came up with was like a bungalow within the larger house. You enter through a small office space that's furnished like a sitting room, with a skirted table as a desk. Files, fabric swatches, and other materials are hidden away in wicker boxes organized neatly on shelves. Beyond the office is a long gallery that's flooded with natural light, thanks to windows that look onto the garden. The hallway is decorated with art and antiques, lamps and rugs, and has cantaloupe-colored walls. The idea is that you're slowly transitioning from a quasi-public space to the inner sanctum, my actual bedroom.

I like to think of it as a living room that happens to have a bed in it. And that's really what it is, with several seating areas anchored by

OPPOSITE AND ABOVE: The master suite functions like its own little house within a house, and the gallery hallway leads from public to private space with antiques and art slowly drawing the eye to the inner sanctum; it includes a minibar and coffee station so I don't have to hike to the kitchen for refreshments. FOLLOWING PAGES: The bed, where I often work à la Edith Wharton, is a sanctuary, complete with a pleated rosette canopy.

143

side chairs, tufted settees, and armchairs; a cocktail table; a Louis XV bureau plat to work at when I'm not working in bed, which I do 90 percent of the time like Edith Wharton (only without the Pulitzer Prize–winning body of work, ha!); commodes and consoles; and an armoire. If you're going to use a bedroom for working, you have to be able to draw clear boundaries. At the end of the day, I put everything away in the armoire and close it up tight, so I can truly shut down. Out of sight, out of mind. Let the unwinding begin!

When I have close friends over, guess where we always congregate? The settees and armchairs are plush and welcoming, and we can mix cocktails at the minibar in the gallery, then tuck in and be completely at home in an ample space that's intimate and cocooning and feels like the safest, most comfy place in the world. Now obviously, I'm not hosting business dinners or I-barely-know-you acquaintances in there, but for my tight inner circle, it's heaven.

Of course, that's doubly true when I'm just entertaining me, myself, and I. As a sanctuary, I wanted my bedroom to have everything I love. I was obsessed with having a view of the gardens and the pool from my bed, because as much as I love interiors, it's gardens where I feel most at home. I had a fantasy of needing to walk only a few steps in the morning to swim in the pool, as it is what I do for exercise most days. French doors opening onto a small porch and the garden beyond gave me both.

Aesthetically, I also wanted a room that felt really light. The palette is dominated by the colors I love. It's basically a watered-down version of the scheme in the living room. All of the fabrics and the wallpaper inhabit that color family, with a latticework wallpaper grounding the room, a retro-chic chintz tumbling all over the upholstery, gleaming duchesse satin and tassels on the bed canopy, more satin with ruffles and pleats as curtains for the French doors, and a melon-pink hue reflecting flattering warm light off of the ceiling. A leopard-print carpet grounds all the fluff with a strong dose of dark color and a cushy, hug-your-bare-toes effect. As I said above, I'm happiest in gardens—this room is like living in a greenhouse that has a ball gown on.

The supporting spaces in the master suite are as much a sanctuary as the bedroom, with a strong framework grounded in function that's so necessary for good design. Following the indoor-garden theme, the bathroom is my version of an outdoor spa. First, an

PREVIOUS PAGES, OPPOSITE, AND ABOVE: The design concept for the bedroom was "a ball gown in a greenhouse," with trellis wallpaper, duchesse satin, and chintz in coordinating shades of watery aqua and melon pink.

The space actually has to fulfill a variety of functions—as a home office, a living room annex, and an actual refuge when I need some downtime—and with multiple workstations and plenty of storage, it actually performs quite well for such seemingly disparate purposes.

If you work from home, it's easy to feel like you're always "on," so at the end of the day, I put everything away in the armoire. With such a fizzy palette and materials, the room needed something to ground it, which a leopard-print carpet does literally, introducing a dark shade that sacrifices nothing in the way of glamour.

PREVIOUS PAGES: Artwork mingles with mementos and family photos around a gilt-wood Regency mirror; I use the Chinese export porcelain plate as a makeshift jewelry stand.
RIGHT: Multiple seating groups give me the option to host meetings with my design staff or hang out when I have just a couple of close friends over.

Used on walls, curtains, and upholstery, an indienne-style print is a unifying design motif in the master bathroom, which adjoins the bedroom via the walk-in closet. The encaustic tiles on the heated floor were an inexpensive alternative to marble that I actually like better because they feel soft and warm underfoot.

indienne-style blue-and-white floral wallpaper and matching fabric cover all the walls and most of the upholstery; it was also used for the curtains framing the bathtub. There you go: instant romance and cohesion with the added effect of a walled garden. The floors are covered in encaustic tiles. To be perfectly honest, marble was just not in the budget. But it was the kind of compromise that ends up being a victory, because encaustic tiles gave me something marble never could: a soft tactility that's hard to beat under bare feet as well as conductivity that makes them cool in the summer and warm in the winter. (And while we're on the subject of bathroom floors, do yourself a favor and always find a way to heat them.) A Venetian mirror above a Deco-style vanity gave me the dose of elegance I needed. There's also ample seating. Here's another good tip: give a big bathroom plenty of seating so loved ones can visit with you while you put on makeup or fix your hair; you will always have a comfortable place to perch while you slip on shoes or draw a bath. With orchids floating in the air like butterflies, the space acts as the world's most glamorous indoor patio.

The walk-in is the closet of my inner clotheshorse's dreams. Here I gained loads of traction from simple, inexpensive ideas. All of the clothing hangs from essentially reinforced curtain rods made by the ironworker I use for my curtain hardware. Shoes sit on open shelves constructed from plywood and then painted. (My philosophy for clothes storage is the same one I have for china storage—if you can't see it, you won't use it.) The walls are in a Benjamin Moore shade I custom matched to my favorite lipstick. And I have to confess that when the paint first went up without any of the furnishings or art, for the first time in my life I thought I'd made a terrible mistake. It looked like a bad neon crayon. But I know that a powerful color needs a lot of layering to tame it. It took all I had to follow my instinct and stay the course. I just kept adding stuff: off-the-shelf mirrored dressers that I pushed together and topped with a piece of plywood wrapped in leftover fabric and covered with a pane of glass; a run-of-the-mill Regency-style armoire I lacquered that same lipstick shade; and most importantly, art. None of it is terribly important, but the idea is that I rotate pieces in and out, and when they are hung salon-style, they elevate the entire space and put that strident color right in its place. The pièce de résistance is a large-scale fashion photograph hung above another mirrored dresser that combines red and coral tones with blue and wicker and pulls the entire scheme together.

163

BREAKFAST ON THE BEDROOM PATIO

The first thing I do in the morning when I get up is fling open the curtains to my bedroom patio. When it's warm enough, it's my favorite place to sit and drink my morning coffee. It's like a second living room, really. It's guarded on either side with skirted console tables, which are great for storing extra candles, clippers, and other indoor-outdoor miscellany. For a little bit of sparkle I created trellis-framed mirrors, the easiest and most inexpensive thing in the world to do by laying borders of painted Home Depot lattice over simple mirrors. There are hanging baskets of ferns, a cast-iron table and grotto chairs, and painted cement floors that mimic a rug.

Unsurprisingly, it's also one of my favorite places to feed people, especially when the weather is fine. For weekend guests, I'll often shake up the formula of breakfast in the kitchen with a come-as-you-are buffet from which they can serve themselves on their own time. I'll just let them know the night before that the meal will be on the patio, often followed by a morning dip in the pool or leisurely catching a little bit of Vitamin D.

Breakfast doesn't have to be anything complicated. My go-to is a serve-yourself granola-and-yogurt spread. As with everything else, the key is in the presentation. I'll fill a silver punch bowl with ice, stock it with individual-sized containers of yogurt—I particularly like the fancy ones that come in the little glass jars—and set it on one of the consoles beneath the trellised mirrors along with a basket of flowers. A blue-and-white soup tureen holds sliced fruit and berries. The granola comes out in the glass container I normally store it in (not everything on the table has to be fancy, and it's actually better if it's not, because it loosens things up) with a soup ladle for serving. A wicker-wrapped carafe gets filled with hot coffee, while I use china to match the soup tureen for creamer and sugar. Add in a vase of flowers for the table and a whip-stitched blue-and-white Lithuanian tablecloth that I found on one of my travels, and breakfast is served. My guests never need to know that I rolled out of bed only twenty minutes before them.

To shake up breakfast for overnight guests when the weather is nice, I'll arrange a buffet on my bedroom patio for a charming, open-air change of scenery that takes two seconds to set up.

Blue and white is a fresh combination that always looks right, especially at the beginning of the day. I try to use all of my serving pieces, no matter how old-fashioned they might seem, and a soup tureen makes the perfect presentation for cut fruit.

EASTER LUNCH ON THE PATIO

Easter is probably my favorite holiday. Winter is finally over, and everything is sprouting—it's a season of rebirth. It's festive but also a bit formal, so there's a reason to go the extra mile and do something a little more elevated. In my case, that means pulling out all the stops in full color. A big arrangement of peonies, roses, and hydrangeas that I put in a silver punch bowl gave me my cues, prompting a bright magenta tablecloth, magenta-trimmed napkins, and a blowsy chinoiserie chintz underskirt. The china drew in the lilac tones in the arrangement with more painted flowers and plates and chargers with small-scale patterns in similar shades. When you're building your table, think of blending colors like you would in a painting—and don't be a stickler about everything matching exactly. Similar tones in warmer or cooler gradations will always work together.

If the gathering is more formal, it's nice to use place cards, even if it's a small event. Your guests will know you thought of them and where they'd be most comfortable. It's also a way to give the table more dimension, because you can anchor the place cards with something interesting or appealing. I've used shells, stones, and silver holders, but you can use pretty much anything. In this case, I filled wooden decorative nests with marble Easter eggs I bought on a whim and filed away in my china closet, not knowing that one day, they would be the icing on the cake of a very pretty Easter table. Collect with abandon, and your collections will pay you back.

And don't forget to decorate the "walls" in your outdoor rooms. Because of the way the master bedroom addition extended down one side of the house, it left a large expanse of blank wall near the pool that was giving me the heebie-jeebies. Leaving it bare felt like a waste of square footage, but I didn't want plain old flower beds there. Luckily, I got an idea while I was on vacation in Italy. The proprietors of a restaurant we had lunch at had used terra-cotta pots to delineate part of the dining room. My mind immediately started spinning, and by the time I got home, I'd figured it out: I could use terra-cotta pots like window boxes, and if I planted a climbing vine such as jasmine, I could espalier it and create a pattern (my favorite!) on the wall like a 3D wallpaper. It zones off a part of the patio in a natural way, creating this elegant nook for small-scale entertaining.

OPPOSITE AND FOLLOWING PAGES: My Easter table is unapologetically joyful, with a bright magenta tablecloth layered over a romantic chintz. I played up the blossom-strewn fabric with floral china layered on top of geometric patterns that contain the same colors.

Garden Party

In Atlanta, you can be outside for a party at least nine months out of the year. My garden is absolutely one of my primary staging grounds for entertaining. I treat it like an extension of the house and think its different parts are just like rooms—except instead of walls, floors, paint, and furniture, they're made up of trees and shrubs, gravel and grass, flowers and leaves and sky. When I plotted the garden out, I thought of it very literally in this way, as a series of venues for entertaining that would serve different purposes, and I designed accordingly: there's the pleached-hornbeam section that skews a little bit formal, the colorful *potager* that's more charming and casual, the kitchen annex that's like an extended dining room, and the pool patio with beds of all-white blooms that's so elegant in the spring when everything is in flower.

When it comes to entertaining, a garden gives you the kind of magic that no room, no matter how well decorated, ever could. It's an embarrassment of sensory riches you can't reproduce indoors: the crunch of gravel underfoot, the sweet scent of roses or jasmine or gardenias, the tickle of the breeze across the back of your neck, twinkling stars above. Any lunch, dinner, or cocktail hour automatically feels more special in the open air.

Of course, entertaining is just the tip of the iceberg. I'm a sun hat–wearing, weeding-for-fun, pruning, shearing, mulching, troweling, potting, propagating, dyed-in-the-wool Southern gardener. I'm not only interested in the way my garden *looks*, I actually need it to work for me. You want to know what real luxury is? Walking into a room bursting with flowers that you've clipped from your own backyard or slicing into a tomato still warm from the sun that slants across your raised vegetable beds.

ABOVE: Pea gravel brings a sense of color and texture and is a great unifying garden element. OPPOSITE: The secret to a lawn that stays green all year long around the pool? ForeverLawn. Most people don't even realize it's not real, and it's a no-brainer in terms of maintenance, good for the environment and well, always green! FOLLOWING PAGES: The master wing accesses the garden directly.

I don't care how inviting your house is, when it comes to entertaining, nothing beats the great outdoors for full-on, all-five-senses magic.

I *have* to have fresh flowers in the house. And there's nothing like trekking out after coffee to see what's good to connect you to the garden and make you present—it's like my morning meditation. In fact, I planted so well for cutting, at certain times of the year I could probably open a flower shop. I have dogwoods, azaleas, gardenias, oakleaf hydrangeas, 'Limelight' hydrangeas, crape myrtle, snowball viburnum, spirea, jasmine, and roses. During fall and winter, there are other types of greenery to collect. A clutch of autumn branches is stunning in the fall, and guess what? Evergreens aren't called evergreens for nothing.

My kitchen garden is a thing of wonder. I've planted prolifically here, too: raspberries, blueberries (which I let go wild along the property line, because they aren't so pretty—but they do make great pie, and I'll scramble up the slope to pick them), squash, zucchini, melons, okra, asparagus, too many different kinds of tomatoes to count, kumquats, Meyer lemons, and herbs galore. It's so convenient and inspiring to have a bounty of produce literally steps from the kitchen door. I'll go out there and see what's good and think, Oh the mint's doing great, it's time to have people over for mojitos; or the scented geranium looks lovely, maybe I'll make a cake; or the tomatoes are ripe for a sandwich, I'll have to get so-and-so over, they're her favorite! I love this ritualistic aspect of entertaining: the planning, the imagining, and then the clipping, the cooking, the putting it all together. What I love even more is that, since the garden is hidden from the view of neighbors, I can do 85 percent of my gardening in my pajamas, essentially without ever having to leave the house.

ABOVE: In the *potager*, a clutch of blackberries grows through the pergola, which works like a *tuteur* for climbing plants and makes the garden ornament functional as well as decorative. OPPOSITE AND FOLLOWING PAGES: Planting beds in the main garden are delineated by limestone-brick and boxwood hedges and planted with white-blooming flowers.

176

(*Gracious Living*)
SOW AND SOW

In my last house, the *potager* was out the mudroom door, across the driveway, and up some stairs about a million miles away from the kitchen. It felt like an afterthought and was about as far from convenient to the actual act of cooking as you could get. This time, I wanted a *potager* that felt incorporated into the main house, right off the kitchen so I could actually access it without a hike. I sited it right outside the breakfast room, which I use all the time, so it also needed to be a worthy visual focal point.

The problem with that, of course, is that vegetable gardens are not always so attractive. The mechanics of actually growing things—and the cycles those growing things go through—can be a tad unsightly. My solution? To disguise some of those rough edges with structure that would stay pretty all the time and then add in enough verdant layers to round out the whole thing: herbs and flowers for cutting, ferns, and lemon and orange trees in pots that move inside in the winter.

I found the pergola at a junk stall one day as I was leaving Scott Antique Markets in Atlanta. It was disassembled into a million rusted pieces, but I knew immediately that it was the perfect thing to build the *potager* around. I had it powder-coated in navy blue (the same color as the shutters and wrought-iron garden furniture) and then plotted it out as a centerpiece with built-in raised brick beds around it. The whole area is on an axis with both the breakfast room indoors and the hornbeam garden and kitchen patio outside. (I used spray paint and laid down broomsticks directly on the dirt to get a feel for it and show the contractors what I was going for.)

The best part is that the pergola is not only a pretty ornament with a chinoiserie spirit that thoroughly grounds the *potager*, it's also supremely functional. It works like a *tuteur*, so I can grow things vertically on it: cucumbers and squash, climbing beans, other vines. At the height of the growing season, it's a beautiful place to host a meal.

The *potager* is defined by a vintage chinoiserie pergola that I found rusted and in pieces while leaving Scott Antique Markets in Atlanta one day. I had it powder-coated navy blue, built raised vegetable beds around it, and made it a focal point.

(*Stylish Entertaining*)
TOMATO-SEASON LUNCH

It was the middle of summer, and the tomatoes were bursting. In the South, a fresh tomato sandwich in July is like eggnog at Christmas, and sharing your crop is reason enough for a party. The best recipes keep things simple: I usually slice and salt the tomatoes and then weight them between paper towels for a couple hours to drain excess juice. Then I put them between supermarket white bread that I've cut with a biscuit round, add some salt and pepper, a skim of mayo, a few leaves of freshly picked basil, and I'm done. It really doesn't get much better than that.

Iced tea as an accompaniment was a natural choice, and homemade is the best—I don't understand why people don't make it more. I brew a concentrate with two cups of boiling water, a few tea bags, some mint, and a stick of sugarcane that sweetens it *just* a bit, let it sit to reach room temperature then dilute it with cold water. Serving it in vintage glasses with the sandwiches gave me an excuse to use silver iced-tea spoons I got on eBay. I love task-specific silver; it takes entertaining to the next level.

I'm generally not a big fan of yellow, but I love my vintage set of yellow cabbageware because it's so unexpected and it illustrates my point about collecting: if you gather up what you love and store it in a way that's accessible, you will use it and your table settings will be more inventive for it. The sandwiches just popped against that bright shade. As for an arrangement, I'm not a planner. I'm not going to call up the florist and order a bouquet, especially for something thrown together like this. I simply pulled what was good from the herb and flower beds: basil, rosemary, marigolds, some dribs of geranium. The goal was to make an arrangement that felt as carefree as the afternoon. If you loosen up about those kinds of details, your guests will relax, too. I'll take impromptu and heartfelt over preplanned and overdone any day.

OPPOSITE AND PREVIOUS PAGES: The garden, especially the *potager*, is endless inspiration for entertaining—what else are you going to do with a bumper crop of tomatoes but make sandwiches for a crowd so that everyone can savor a true Southern delicacy?

(*Stylish Entertaining*)
EAT-YOUR-VEGETABLES SUPPER

Magic happens when you nurture something from a seed or seedling into something edible, and I am a passionate gardener. Honestly, if I weren't a designer, I'd probably be a farmer. I grow so much, and since I'm only one woman, I'm a firm believer in the idea that food just tastes better when you share it. So when the vegetables were popping, I designed a light summer supper around the harvest.

I really wanted to showcase my handiwork, so I made the menu reflect that. The star dish was a crudités centerpiece that doubled as decoration and the main course: basically guests pulled from a cork bowl in which I'd arranged my prettiest produce to create their own *salades composées* with homemade aioli. I love to serve this kind of interactive dish at a dinner party. It's like theater, and it forces people to engage in a hands-on way, passing the endive and the tomatoes. And you don't have to grow it all yourself to pull off something like this—the farmers market or the grocery store has plenty of veggies, too.

The rest of the food was garden-centric as well: caponata and green-bean salads made with the homegrown stuff and an egg salad to round things out. I made my own ginger ale by brewing simple syrup with fresh ginger and adding sparkling water. I also provided vodka so that diners could spike at will.

The place settings raised the stakes a bit. Vintage Limoges china painted with vegetables had the right balance of haute charm. Pairing it with casual bamboo-handled flatware and crisp linen napkins embroidered with more vegetables added a sweet but sophisticated touch and made it feel unbuttoned in a glamorous way. The deepening twilight and the buzz of the garden provided the rest of the enchantment.

OPPOSITE AND FOLLOWING PAGES: Forget farm-to-table dining. With a prolific vegetable garden at home, you can have yard-to-table meals—like a lunch featuring *salade composée* from produce I grew myself—that need very little embellishment to make them sing.

The garden furniture—a mix of vintage wrought-iron pieces and store-bought chaises—was all powder-coated a navy shade so they have my stamp; my kids joke that I'll powder-coat anything that stands still. The Greek-key border around the pool edge echoes a similar edge on the floors in the kitchen.

RIGHT AND FOLLOWING PAGES:
The loggia just off the
living room is another
favorite venue for
entertaining, whether
it's an open-air brunch
featuring my collection
of French majolica or
a festive Mexican-
inspired dinner starring
an Otomi tablecloth.

(*Stylish Entertaining*)
A POOLSIDE FEAST

The pool is my refuge. When I'm home, I start most mornings with a swim. But it also serves a higher purpose in the garden. It's a sculptural focal point equipped with fountains that I can turn on with a switch and when the music's playing outside, you half expect Esther Williams to burst through the deep end. It also divides the garden into zones that I treat like outdoor rooms, especially the grassy rectangular patch outside the master suite, which I deployed as a dining area for a spring supper for a baker's dozen.

I first focused on the food itself. When I'm serving dinner to a lot of people in my own house, I try to appeal to a broad range of tastes and like to think that what I'm really providing is comfort. It's one of the many benefits of entertaining at home. You get to strip away some pretension. No one wants to eat flambéed foie gras balanced on half of a skinned grape. The key word here was *unfussy*: barbecue chicken, grilled asparagus, and a corn salad. But I also made it feel quasi-homemade because my caterer uses my recipes, which is *almost* as good as cooking it all myself. (Tip: make it a point to develop a relationship with your go-to person—it's a really nice touch.)

Otherwise, a seated dinner this large is bound to feel a little formal, and that's OK because you can foster intimacy in other ways, namely the size of the table. I swear by my Coleman folding camping tables because they're a little narrower than you might expect, so people sit closer together. More people with less table between them is always going to mean people talk and interact more. The camping tables are also easy to store, move, and arrange in a whole range of configurations (like the rectangle here), and when covered in a white linen tablecloth and printed damask underskirt, no one can tell anyway. They're an essential part of my arsenal for parties. So are my Chiavari ballroom chairs. I have fifty of them because they stack on one another, take up very little room, and come in handy all the time. My theory is that if you can buy something for essentially the same price as a single rental and you have the space to store it, do it.

The table settings came together around Mottahedeh's Tobacco Leaf china. I use the pattern all the time because it has every color in it—pink, purple, blue, rust, ocher, and green—which makes it so versatile. Play up the rusty tones with orange and red dahlias and mums, and you've got a fall feeling. Play up the greens, pinks, and purples, like we did here with peonies, ranunculus, tulips, and hydrangeas, and you're capturing the height of spring. Emerald-toned flatware and lilac water glasses further played up the jewel tones. The final flourish was long taper candles in etched-crystal hurricane lamps. Dressy, yes, but also incredibly atmospheric.

OPPOSITE, FOLLOWING PAGES, AND PAGES 200-201: I keep an arsenal of folding camping tables that can be deployed in any number of configurations, from a cozy rectangle for eight to a spread for twenty-four. Flowers, napkins, flatware, and glassware echo shades in the china to create a vibrant table that hangs together well.

I always joke that I want a house you can clean with a leaf blower and a hose, and that's what I got with the cabana. I was looking to re-create the idea of a boathouse—something functional but rustic and an escape from the formality of the main house, which is why you'd want to be in a cabana in the first place. I kept saying to the builder, "Don't finish the inside. I want the overhead beams exposed, and I'll just paint it all." He didn't believe me. He kept trying to convince me to air-condition it. Sometimes getting people to leave well enough alone is the hardest thing in the world.

But I knew how I wanted to live out there, and it was not formally. This is a place for ceiling fans and shorts, for enjoying the garden.

Of course, I also wanted a space I could use for a party. A venue like that changes the whole dynamic of an event. There is a sink and counters and shelves for prep work (they double as a second potting area when I'm planting in that side of the garden), a powder room, and iron daybeds with plush cushions deep enough for lounging that can be called into service as banquettes at a dinner party. The atmosphere is light and easy, precisely what you want from a gathering in a garden and definitely the effect I was going for when I invited friends over for a late-summer supper.

At that time of year everyone wants to be outside, but the garden is raggedy and it's hot. Hosting near the pool cools things down and takes the focus off the threadbare gardenia beds. The color white cools things down, too, so I used white tablecloths, white linen napkins, a blue and white–striped underskirt, and the pièce de résistance: big clouds of fluffy white baby's breath gathered in wicker baskets on both ends of the table. Deploying unsung blooms is one of my favorite tricks. Baby's breath used en masse like this is a sleeper hit, unexpected and reminiscent of a lush meadow. (Bunches of branches or leaves would work the same magic.) Also, when you elevate humble things like that, they tend to take the formality down a notch. People relax more.

The rest of the table followed suit, with wicker-wrapped drinking glasses and water carafes, simple wood-handled flatware, and nickel-tipped hurricane lamps. It had such a graceful, barefoot vibe that we may as well have been in Nantucket. As for the food, I've said this before and I'll say it again: easy is always better, and if I don't even have to cook, then it's a home run. It had been a long week, and I was dying to see my friends but not dying to fuss over a hot stove. At the height of summer, no one wants anything fussy anyway. So you know what I did? I made a lush green salad from lettuces, radishes, cucumbers, and tomatoes I had grown myself, and I replated fancy takeout pizza onto a wooden wheel I brought right to the table. Throw in ice-cold bottles of rosé and do you think anyone complained? I'll give you one guess.

OPPOSITE AND PREVIOUS PAGES: The cabana is a pool house, party venue, and auxiliary potting shed complete with its own powder room and wet bar to facilitate serving or cleaning up. It's an open-air pavilion on purpose—air-conditioning would have ruined the mood.

People think baby's breath is unchic, but it gains a stylishness all its own when used en masse and placed front and center—giving the table a down-to-earth charm and upending expectations. Wicker-wrapped serving ware is a breezy but elegant addition.

(*Stylish Entertaining*)
FALL DINNER IN THE HORNBEAM GARDEN

If any space in the garden feels like a room in the literal sense, it's the hornbeam garden located steps above the pool: an elegant swath of lawn surrounded on four sides by a hedge of carefully pleached hornbeam trees, creating a hidden nook surrounded by a cocoon of green that's perfect for more formal entertaining.

All those elements made it an ideal setting for a fall dinner I hosted for a small group of friends. The weather was still pleasant, so it felt like a shame to coop people up indoors, but everyone was back from summer vacations, the kids were back in school, the mood was back to business. (By February that attitude gets old, but in October it's still exciting and part of what makes the fall one of my favorite times of year.)

There's nothing like the juxtaposition of a serious antique in an outdoor setting to upend expectations and establish ambience. Cue the carved Georgian console, which I set up as a bar. It needed nothing but a silver tray and ice bucket to dress it up. The same philosophy holds true for velvet-covered Louis XVI dining chairs, which I borrowed from the dining room. And why not? If Napoleon traveled with a whole suite of serious Empire furniture that was set up for him in a tent, I can certainly drag a few chairs across the lawn to achieve the same kind of elegance. Trust me: when you sit on a real dining chair for dinner in the open air, you know you're in for something special.

A cast-iron statue of a stag (I *do* live in Buckhead) that stands sentry in the garden gave me my woodland theme: antler-handled flatware, an antler candelabra at the bar, china painted with butterflies, and cocktail napkins embroidered with feathers. I used a burgundy charger to play up the rich, dusky fall tones in the late-season sunflowers I arranged with hydrangeas in a silver punch bowl for the centerpiece. For an eclectic, unexpected touch, I used an ikat tablecloth and bright embroidered monogrammed napkins—the mix of patterns feels collected (which gibes with the antiques), and the splash of color kept the scene from tipping into somber.

OPPOSITE AND FOLLOWING PAGES: An antique console and dining chairs I pulled from indoors elevate supper in the hornbeam garden, where pleached trees make you feel as if you're in a green cocoon. Late-season blooms and an ikat tablecloth give the scene just the right pop of color.

PICNIC ON THE FRONT LAWN

One of the good things about buying a house with a garden that was neglected and overgrown is that I didn't have to feel bad about ripping everything out—I had no choice. To create privacy, I planted a hedge of arborvitae to screen a large portion of the front lawn from view. On the side I created another hedge, this one with more flowering shrubs and plants than you can shake a stick at, all in shades of white. There are azaleas, camellias, jasmine, dogwoods, snowball viburnums, spirea, and all kinds of hydrangeas. From spring into early fall, it's bursting with flowers. When the bloom season starts, it's a stunning place to entertain guests and an ideal spot for a picnic.

I had in my mind the kind of lunch you might see on *Downton Abbey* with a crew of liveried servants. I may not have an army of butlers and footmen, but I have imagination in spades, and sometimes all it takes is inspiration like that to get you going. I took a sixty-inch round folding table and threw an Indian scenic chintz tablecloth over it. Actual Victorian wrought-iron garden chairs were a shoo-in for seating. By now, you know I don't do paper plates: I deployed embroidered-linen napkins, china with a floral pattern, simple wineglasses and goblets, and my trusty bamboo flatware. Wicker baskets held fruit (pretty on the table and good enough to eat), and I clipped hydrangeas from the hedge for a big crystal vase.

Overflowing peaches at the grocery store gave me an idea for homemade peach ice cream, which is just about the best thing in the world in Georgia in the summer. I spent most of my energy there—one special treat like that is really all you need to distinguish a meal you serve for friends. I pureed more peaches for Bellinis. Everything else was straightforward and appealing—grilled chicken paillard, a green-bean salad—the kind of make-ahead stuff that's easy to serve from a platter and enjoyable at room temperature.

The front lawn is screened from the street by landscaping, making it a great locale for a picnic inspired by British costume dramas, complete with china, linens, wicker baskets, a chintz tablecloth, and tole lanterns for an extra dose of romance.

Pajama Games

he second floor of the house is the kids' domain. It has their bedrooms, which double as guest rooms when they're away (two have already flown the nest). As young adults, when they were all in residence, I wanted them to have a sense of privacy. I always jokingly said that the middle part of the house could blow up and I wouldn't even know it. Keeping the kids' spaces separate also allowed me to avoid being the annoying mother, constantly haggling for them to clean up. Out of sight, out of mind.

A bedroom is a bedroom is a bedroom, even if it's meant for a child. I gave them all mini versions of what I had: large closets and bathrooms, a desk for them to work at, and sitting areas where they can read or hang out with friends. The setup makes the rooms especially useful when they're called into service as guest quarters, because visitors have everything they need and feel self-sufficient and tucked away. The rooms were decorated with the kids' tastes in mind, yes, but also with an eye for longevity and timelessness so that they could eventually suit that other purpose. That approach worked for the kids anyway. They are their mother's children and have a healthy appreciation for design and collecting that they've been absorbing since birth through osmosis. There's nothing juvenile about these spaces.

My son Preston, who still lives at home, probably caught the collecting bug the most. He loves his heirlooms as much as I do and has a thing for vintage silver and textiles and a yen for antiques; he also likes to display everything, as I do. In his room, we dove into a masculine campaign style that felt classic. I wanted the antique furniture we chose—a highboy, a campaign chest, and a chair—to feel fresh,

ABOVE: In my son Preston's bathroom, encaustic tiles in a rhombille pattern give a vanity fashioned from an antique commode an updated edge; an antique side chair doubles as a surface for towels and accessories.

OPPOSITE: A tented bed and antiques such as a chest and a highboy play up a campaign theme while a rich navy blue on the walls brings a freshness to mahogany tones.

so I chose a deep navy hue as a backdrop, which sets off those burnished-mahogany tones handsomely. A ticking-stripe bed-curtain (the easiest thing to install with curtain dowels) lightens up the scene so it doesn't feel too stuffy (he is a teenager, after all). I used a blue-and-white toile print for the Roman shades, his headboard, and the bed and table skirts for the same reason: just the slightest touch of femininity loosens the room up.

An extra bedroom on the second floor was designed specifically as a guest room, and my approach was bright, simple, and layered. It's basically a medley of stripes and ginghams in red, white, blue, and brown. It's smaller than the other rooms, but more bed-curtains installed here make the most of the tight space, so it feels cozy rather than claustrophobic. And everyone should have at least one guest room with twin beds, because they give you that extra layer of flexibility in accommodating different configurations of visitors, from babies to teens.

My daughter, Carlyle, is the quirky free spirit of the bunch, and she wanted a space that was happy and whimsical. Oddly enough, she initially asked me for an all-white bedroom, and I was like, "Um, that's *not* going to happen." But she does love the color blue (like me!), and we narrowed it down to a scheme of aqua, red, and white. It didn't take long to convince her of the room's major design statement: a bright and graphic red-and-white Sister Parish print we used on the walls, bed canopy, table skirt, and upholstery. An allover pattern like that in a small space instantly gives a room cohesion. To keep the canopy from feeling too sweet, I had it fabricated from plumbing pipe that I painted matte nickel for an industrial effect. A zebra-patterned rug grounded the room and brought in a retro-chic El Morocco vibe. Artwork meaningful to her hung salon-style capped the whole thing with sophistication.

My oldest, Emerson, is much more reverent about objects but prefers a stripped-down approach. He appreciates things, but he doesn't want a lot of them—my connoisseur. His room has a clubby gentleman's vibe: a Harris plaid on the headboard and table skirts, coordinating small-scale wool checks on armchairs, shed antlers, and chocolate-brown walls. A lampshade covered in pheasant feathers and an antelope-print rug provide a slight English-country subtext. He's into music, so framed vintage albums and portraits of musicians give that sensibility a youthful edge.

PREVIOUS PAGES: Twin beds in a guest room give you extra flexibility in accommodating visitors, from toddlers to teens. ABOVE AND OPPOSITE: In the guest bath, the pattern on the shower tiles mimics the gingham check on the bed linens reflected in the mirror, while Roman shades and sconces reprise red tones elsewhere; the vanity is made from brass plumbing pipe.

218

A red-and-white Sister Parish print defines the room of my daughter, Carlyle, combining with aqua highlights and a zebra-print rug to furnish a glamorous El Morocco vibe. To cut the sweetness factor by a notch, I fabricated the canopy from plumbing pipe painted matte nickel finish—just that little industrial nod balances out the fizz.

ABOVE AND OPPOSITE: To establish a clubby English-country vibe in my son Emerson's room, I used wool plaids, coordinating small-scale windowpane checks, an antelope-print rug, and a pheasant-feather lampshade. The bathroom riffs on the same tones with a vanity composed of antiques.

Child's Play

If the grown-ups need a space to entertain, then the kids do, too—think souped-up rec room that the adults can also co-opt for cutthroat Ping-Pong tournaments.

I didn't want my basement to feel like a basement, and I certainly didn't want this one to look like what it did when I first encountered it: dark, decrepit, and haunted. And just as I needed staging grounds like the library, living room, and family room for my entertaining, I wanted a space my kids could devote to theirs. Think a private club with Ping-Pong and pool tables that could stand up to rowdy teenagers—and could also welcome the occasional adult or two during holiday tournaments, one of our favorite Christmas pastimes.

I upholstered a sofa in vintage Hudson's Bay blankets (talk about a performance fabric!), and that inspired the wall treatment. Because the architecture had unavoidable awkward elevation drops, I embraced and highlighted them by continuing the blanket stripes up the wall. The blankets inspired the color scheme: red and yellow walls and a red plaid carpet. It's cozy and colorful for the kids.

I had my stroke of genius for the floors of the wet bar—a rec-room-adjacent space that's a strictly juice-and-soda venue unless adults are hanging around. By the time I got to decorating the downstairs area, I'd run out of budget for tiles, and seeing a penny on a sidewalk gave me an idea. What if I floored the space in hundreds of one-cent pieces? It was much easier than you'd think. I attached them to standard double-sided tiling mesh, installed them with black grout, and then covered them in polyurethane. It's cute, it's fun, it's cheap, and it's held up like iron.

ABOVE: By the time I got to the basement, I'd run out of budget for tiles, so I paved the floor of the wet bar in pennies. The rec room isn't just my kids' domain; I'll often load the bar cart with adult refreshments and entertain my own friends with a rousing game of Ping-Pong or pool.
OPPOSITE: I used vintage Hudson's Bay blankets to upholster the sofa and continued the striped pattern on the wall and ceiling to highlight—instead of fight—awkward architecture that I couldn't do anything about.

The Heart of the House

hen it comes to real estate, some people go gaga for four-car garages or his-and-hers bathrooms or closets big enough to waltz in. And although I agree that all of those things are very nice, what really floats my boat are service areas: mudrooms, flower and potting rooms, linen closets. And don't even get me started on laundry rooms. Why? Because while most of the time marquee spaces like master suites get the lion's share of attention, all those flashy rooms aren't worth their square footage if they don't have service areas to support them.

Can you unload your groceries without having to trek through the entire house? Is there an ample, well-lit space, complete with a deep sink, in which you can pot plants you want to bring in from the garden or where you can arrange flowers you buy at the farmers market? Do you have a dedicated laundry space big enough to comfortably handle all you regularly throw at it, with roomy areas to fold and iron and racks with drip pans for hanging hand-washed garments to dry? Do you have multiple linen closets near bedrooms for easy access and change-outs? Workhorse spaces like these are the unsung heroes of well-run houses everywhere because they let you get down to the nitty-gritty of living— by which I mean washing, cleaning, arranging, and prepping—in efficient, practical ways that keep messes to a minimum and far from prying eyes and make a comfortable, clean house feel like magic.

Since we're talking about my dream house here, when I was plotting out renovations, the answer to all of the above questions had to be yes. It started with not just a mudroom but a mud hall that connects the garage to the kitchen (grocery unloading is a cinch), then a potting and flower-arranging room, a powder room with access to the garden

OPPOSITE AND ABOVE: Vintage engravings and Gullah woven Charleston baskets hang on the wall of the mud hall, while settees covered in trapunto-stitched chintz slipcovers offer a cushy perch to finish a call or get organized. If you decorate back-of-house spaces with the same attention you give the living room, rolling up your sleeves won't feel like too much of a chore. FOLLOWING PAGES: The potting area has its own powder room with direct access to the garden, so mud never comes very far into the house; the potting area itself has a deep and wide apron sink and plenty of open shelving to store pots, vases, and other materials.

(muddy Wellies never get beyond it), and cabinets organized by purpose, from pet care to storage of oversize receptacles for flowers. And if you think a service area means utilitarian decor, think again. The hallways are painted the same shade of blue as the kitchen for cohesion and furnished with comfy settees covered in trapunto-stitched chintz. Big woven-seagrass baskets catch overflow sports equipment or miscellaneous effluvia; daintier Gullah woven baskets from Charleston line the walls of an additional office area.

The potting room's deep terra-cotta apron sink is big enough for my largest vases; the room also features framed botanical engravings, open shelves for pots, and cubbies with baskets of garden shears and clippers. I'll come in from the market with big bundles of flowers and plop them there and get to work; arranging blooms in that room is one my greatest regular joys.

My laundry room is another point of pride. Basically, I could run a hotel with it. Form follows function here. The floors are done with a checkerboard star pattern in cork, which is easy on the feet. I covered an island in a ticking stripe that works for ironing and folding and conceals storage underneath. There are two washers and two dryers, a hanging area with drainage for delicates to dry, and a deep stainless steel sink for handwashing. Laundry and cleaning supplies are stored in baskets and organized on trays. For a decorative touch, I added vintage soap-ad posters and a sleight-of-hand design flourish: I had a carpenter bevel the edges of standard two-by-four blocks of wood and lined the walls like wainscoting. It looks like the rusticated facades of Renaissance palaces—how's that for elevating folding and sorting?

My approach with linen closets is to have multiple small ones with ample open shelves, each dedicated to its own room or pair of rooms at the most. It's just the easiest way to keep organized and ensure that the striped sheets that match the color scheme of my daughter Carlyle's room don't wind up on my son Emerson's bed (which usually doubles as a guest room, since he's mostly flown the coop). Sheets, pillowcases, and duvets are all stored as sets—rather than individually—so that suites of things stay together. Otherwise they get mixed into the wrong rotation, and untangling it is a headache. I like monogrammed towels for the same reason—it's easy to tell where they're supposed to go. I store cleaning supplies here, too, and beauty products such as candles, toothpaste, and extra toothbrushes in baskets to keep things neat. Labels ensure that my housekeeper, Maria (another unsung hero!), and I stay right on track.

ABOVE: Baskets in linen closets near guest rooms organize toiletries and accessories for easy refills when we're hosting. OPPOSITE: Linen closets are also each dedicated to their own rooms, with sheets organized in sets. FOLLOWING PAGES: Vintage soap posters and geometric cork floors mean laundry gets done without too much drudgery.

Resources

CANDLES, FLOWERS, AND STATIONERY

Creative Candles
creativecandles.com

Dixie Design
dixie-design.com

High Camp
highcampsupply.com

La Petite Abeille
thelittlebee.net

Mrs. John L. Strong
mrsstrong.com

The Printery
iprintery.com

Renny and Reed Flowers
rennyandreed.com

Tom Mathieu
tommathieu.com

Weston Farms
westonfarms.com

F AND F (FABRICS AND FURNISHINGS)

Ainsworth-Noah
ainsworth-noah.com

Annie Selke/Dash & Albert Rugs
annieselke.com

Ballard Designs
ballarddesigns.com

Bielecky Brothers
bieleckybrothers.com

Carolina Irving Textiles
carolinairvingtextiles.com

Casa Gusto
getthegusto.com

Christie's
christies.com

Christopher Spitzmiller
christopherspitzmiller.com

Church Mouse
bbts.org/about-us/church-mouse/

Circa Lighting
circalighting.com

Circa Who
circawho.com

Cowtan & Tout
cowtan.com

Currey & Company
curreyandcompany.com

de Gournay
degournay.com

Doyle
doyle.com

Etú Home
etuhome.com

Fabricut, Stroheim, and Vervain
fabricut.com

Florida Regency
floridaregency.com

Fromental
fromental.co.uk

Hudson Valley Lighting
hudsonvalleylighting.hvlgroup.com

Kravet, Lee Jofa,
and Brunschwig & Fils
kravet.com

KRB
krbnyc.com

Lisa Fine Textiles
lisafinetextiles.com

Mainly Baskets
mainlybaskets.com

Mecox
mecox.com

Oomph
oomphhome.com

Parc Monceau
parcmonceauatl.com

Phillip Jeffries
phillipjeffries.com

Pierre Frey
pierrefrey.com

Ralph Lauren Home
ralphlaurenhome.com

Scalamandré
scalamandre.com

Schumacher
fschumacher.com

Schuyler Samperton Textiles
schuylersampertontextiles.com

Scott Antique Markets
scottantiquemarket.com

Serena & Lily
serenaandlily.com

The Shade Store
theshadestore.com

Sister Parish Design
sisterparishdesign.com

Sotheby's
sothebys.com

St. Frank
stfrank.com

Stair
stairgalleries.com

Stark
starkcarpet.com

Theodore Alexander
theodorealexander.com

Thibaut
thibautdesign.com

Tommy Mitchell
tommymitchellcompany.com

Travis & Company
travisandcompany.com

Valley Attic
valleyattic.com

Wendover Art
wendoverart.com

OUTDOOR

Brown Jordan
brownjordan.com

McKinnon and Harris
mckinnonharris.com

Pennoyer Newman
pennoyernewman.com

Sunbrella
sunbrella.com

Woodard
woodard-furniture.com

PAINT

Benjamin Moore
benjaminmoore.com

Farrow & Ball
farrow-ball.com

Fine Paints of Europe
finepaintsofeurope.com

TABLEWARE AND LINENS

Cabana
cabanagloballuxe.com

Callidus
calliduspalmbeach.com

Cap Deco
capdeco-france.com

Courtland & Co.
courtlandandco.com

D. Porthault Paris
dporthaultparis.com

Danielle Rollins
danielledrollins.com

Dear Keaton
dearkeaton.com

Dior Maison
dior.com

The Enchanted Home
enchantedhome.com

Fête Home
fetehome.com

Fiona Finds
fionafinds.co.uk

Hotel Silver
hotelsilver.net

India Amory
indiaamory.com

Julia B.
juliab.com

Juliska
juliska.com

Kassatly's
kassatlys.com

La Gallina Matta
lagallinamatta.com

La Rochère
larochere-na.com

La Tuile a Loup
latuilealoup.com/home.html

The Lacquer Company
thelacquercompany.com

Leontine Linens
leontinelinens.com

Léron
leron.com

Leta Austin Foster
letaaustinfoster.com

Loretta Caponi
lorettacaponi.it

Loulou La Dune
loulouladune.com

Margot Larkin
margotlar.com

Martinuzzi
011-39-041-522-5068

Mary Mahoney
marymahoney.com

Matouk
matouk.com

Moda Operandi
modaoperandi.com/home

Once Milano
oncemilano.com

Peacock Alley
peacockalley.com

Pioneer Linens
pioneerlinens.com

Ralph Lauren Home
ralphlaurenhome.com

Replacements, Ltd.
replacements.com

Saban Glass
sabanglassware.com

Scully & Scully
scullyandscully.com

Sue Fisher King
suefisherking.com

Talmaris
talmaris.paris@gmail.com

Walker Valentine
walkervalentine.com

William Yeoward
williamyeoward.com

Williams Sonoma Home
williams-sonoma.com

Acknowledgments

A very special and heartfelt thanks to all of my loving family, my dearest friends, and the talented people who made this book possible.

My mother, Jan Deaton, to whom this book is dedicated, is my raison d'être. She has been my rock, the person who has had the greatest impact on my life. A truly selfless human being, she has been by my side through everything—and there have been a lot of things! Through a combination of pushing me and pulling me, she has taught me to have independence at all costs, given me the perseverance to get through anything and everything, stood by me when my world collapsed, picked me back up when I was under the weight of it, and propped me up enough to think I could climb back on top of it. But most of all, she has always supported me to build my dreams. You've made my children the people they are, and that's the biggest gift of all. And my father, Ron Deaton, for having the patience and time to spend with the children, including hours of Pokémon Go, watching backflips performed on the trampoline, serving as umpire for countless basketball games, and being on call for whatever fix-it task was needed.

My children, Emerson, Carlyle, and Preston, for all of the sacrifices you've made to support me following my dreams and establishing a career. I know this wasn't what any of us had planned, but I appreciate you each rising up to roll along with it. I am extremely proud of the independent, self-sufficient, hardworking, but most of all empathetic and kind, young adults you have become.

My bestest friend and only-in-Italy husband, Billy Ceglia, who is always at the ready, willing, and able. No one can make me laugh like you do. I look forward to wearing matching outfits, Wednesday-night "It must be hot dogs again," and growing old graciously—but maybe not always so gracefully—together. I couldn't get through life, let alone a single day, without my "emotional support friend" and I appreciate your constant and unswerving loyalty.

The "incorrigible" Tom D'Agostino, who can find the right things to say when things don't always seem that way and has shown up in his pink shorts to fix so many of my would-be disasters. Whoever guessed that two years later we would end up where we are? I will always be grateful we had that first drink. I couldn't love you more.

Miles Redd, for believing in me when I didn't believe in myself and lovingly tossing me out of the nest to fly on my own. You have such a talent for recognizing talent and encouraging others to explore their gifts. You have been an incredible friend and treasured mentor WWMD—"What would Miles do?"—is my go-to mantra whenever I encounter a design conundrum and the answer usually magically comes to me in your voice.

In memory of John D. Fornengo, who would have been so proud of this book and enthusiastically worked with me to complete the house, and for Daisy, Augie, and Ally—and dear Pegeen and Paul Bodine, too. And dear

Alessandra Branca, a constant and kind supporter who always has encouraging words.

My goddaughter, Carolina Adams, it seems implausible that any two people could ever have had such a crazy story to tell, but at least we have been through it together. You have been there to give me a reason when I needed one. You will always be close to my heart. Stay scrappy.

To Ginny Brewer and Elizabeth Klump, for thirteen years of cochairing Women of Style and Substance and the countless times you both stepped in because the multiple tasks were greater than my multitasking capabilities.

Leslie Podell, a true artist who has led by the example of following a passion and one who has dropped everything to fly across the country to be with me more than once. And my goddaughter, Madelon, with musical talents to watch.

One of the best friends anyone could ever ask for in the world, Ashley Dabbiere, who has stoically and sometimes stubbornly forced me out of a funk and made my life so much fun.

Alex Gracey and Elle McCloud, because you make my daughter and son happy, and a mother can only be as happy as her least-happy child.

My right arm and the one who keeps it all running so beautifully, Maria Sanchez. The stylist extraordinaire John W. Price. Angela Page, you have weathered the storms, and I appreciate having you on my team and as a friend. For Judy Coleman, who can untangle all the accounting, and for so many errands, and for always being so willing, the ever-cheerful Park Mocke.

Bill Ingram, who helped to interpret my scribblings on the back of a napkin and turn them into the house of my dreams. To Keisha and Daniel Noel, Jada and Tom Loveless, Cynthia Hammond, and Lance Orchid for serving as models when needed and friends always. Ronda Carman and Alex Hitz, who both have listened to my book woes more than I know they wanted to! Dr. Deborah Kelly, for keeping me rocking and rolling no matter where I am.

To Charles Miers and Kathleen Jayes at Rizzoli for helping me make another beautiful book. I hope you will be ready for outing number three because only you could take the things I want to express and turn them into works of art!

To Doug Turshen for being there from day one when I called and said "I have this idea," and who immediately got it, and kept pushing me to do the book I wanted to do. Along with Steve Turner, you had an incredible vision, taking a million random and scattered images and artfully creating this book. To Mario López-Cordero for helping me find the words to tell the story I felt so strongly about sharing and enthusiastically encouraging my talents and gifts.

To Steele Marcoux of *Veranda*, to One Kings Lane, *Atlanta Homes & Lifestyles*, and all of the other magazines and lifestyle blogs that have shared snippets of my home and supported my story.

To the talented photographers Lesley Unruh, Sarah Dorio, Matthew Mead, Melanie Acevedo, and David Christensen.

A sincere thank-you to everyone who bought my first book with Rizzoli, *Soirée: Entertaining with Style*, and to all of the organizations who invited me to speak and everyone who hosted book signings. A little seed was sprouted with that book, which has grown into the burgeoning lifestyle brand that has taken root.

Afterword

Life's too short to spend too much time trying to make everything perfect—it's an impossible task, anyway. That's why I like to think of myself as the Waffle House decorator: I just scatter, smother, and cover. Get the backgrounds as right as you can, invest in the things that bring you joy, and spend the rest of your time making occasions memorable. Whether the methods you use are extravagant or ordinary, I promise the only essential ingredients are making them with and for the people you love.

PHOTOGRAPHY CREDITS

Melanie Acevedo: reverse of front endpaper, 173

© David Christensen: pages 38-41

Sarah Dorio: right endpaper, pages 1, 6, 9 (top right, bottom left and right) 13, 15, 16-17, 18-23, 29-37, 42, 46-49, 52-63, 65, 66, 68-9, 72-78, 82-87, 98, 102, 106, 110-125, 126, 127 (top and bottom left, top right), 128-130, 135-7, 142, 144-5, 147, 150-151, 152-3, 156-7, 166-172, 174-181, 190-195, 202-207, 214-231, reverse of back endpaper

Matthew Mead: left endpaper, pages 4-5, 9 (top left), 14, 24-27, 70-71, 89-91, 100-101, 104-5, 127 (bottom right), 132-3, 134, 139, 165, 182-189, 197-201, 208-213, 238

Lesley Unruh: pages 2-3, 28, 44-45, 50-51, 79-81, 103, 107, 108-9, 131, 140-141, 142-143, 146, 148, 154-155, 158-163, 232-3

Lesley Unruh/One Kings Lane: pages 10, 64, 67, 92-97.

Grateful acknowledgment to One Kings Lane for their support.

First published in the United States
of America in 2020 by
Rizzoli International Publications, Inc.
300 Park Avenue South
New York, NY 10010
www.rizzoliusa.com

Copyright © 2020 Danielle Rollins
Text: Mario López-Cordero
Foreword: Miles Redd

Publisher: Charles Miers
Senior Editor: Kathleen Jayes
Design: Doug Turshen with Steve Turner
Production Manager: Kaija Markoe
Managing Editor: Lynn Scrabis

Printed in Slovenia

2020 2021 2022 2023 / 10 9 8 7 6 5 4 3 2

ISBN: 978-0-8478-6716-5
Library of Congress Control Number: 2020937207

Visit us online:
Facebook.com/RizzoliNewYork
Twitter: @Rizzoli_Books
Instagram.com/RizzoliBooks
Pinterest.com/RizzoliBooks
Youtube.com/user/RizzoliNY
Issuu.com/Rizzoli